# Main Street America
## and The Third World

**The Third World**

# Main Street America

By John Maxwell Hamilton

Foreword by Peter Jennings

# <u>and</u> The Third World

With contributions from *The* (Aurora, Ill.) *Beacon-News*, the *Bristol* (Conn.) *Press, The Christian Science Monitor, The Dallas Morning News*, the *Hattiesburg* (Miss.) *American, The Hopewell* (Va.) *News, The* (Everett, Wash.) *Herald, The Knoxville News-Sentinel*, the *La Crosse* (Wis.) *Tribune*, the (Middletown, N.Y.) *Times Herald-Record*, the *Richmond Times-Dispatch, The Tulsa Tribune,* and WSAZ-TV, Huntington, W. Va.

# Seven Locks Press
Cabin John, Md./Washington, D.C.

Copyright©1986 by Sigma Delta Chi Foundation
*All rights reserved*

**Library of Congress Cataloging-in-Publication Data**

Main Street America and the Third World.

Bibliography: p.
1. Developing countries—Relations—United States.
2. United States— Relations—Developing countries.
3. Developing countries—Foreign opinion, American.
4. Public opinion—United States.
I. Hamilton, John Maxwell.
D888.U6M34  1986    303.4'8273'01734    86-15541
ISBN 0-932020-39-9 (pbk.)


Design by Dan Thomas
Printed by the Maple Press Company, York, Pennsylvania
Manufactured in the United States of America
First edition, October 1986

Map of Third World (pp. ii and iii) courtesy World Bank.

*On the cover:* Main street in La Crosse, Wisconsin, and Dhaka, Bangladesh.
Photos by Dick Riniker, *La Crosse Tribune,* and T. Sennett, World Bank.

# Seven Locks Press
*Publishers*
P.O. Box 27
Cabin John, Md. 20818
202/362-4714

*To my parents*

# Foreword

## By Peter Jennings
Anchor and Senior Editor
ABC World News Tonight

I CAN BE VERY SPECIFIC about why a book such as this is useful and why it behooves journalists, bankers, businesspeople, government officials, educators, and students to read it. I could cite any number of personal experiences, but one will do.

During the ordeal for passengers on board TWA 847, which was hijacked to Beirut in 1985, my news division was in pretty fierce competition with CBS, NBC, and CNN. Eschewing false modesty, I am convinced that the ABC News viewer was better served because the four lead reporters on the story for this network, myself included, knew the backstreets of Beirut, knew the principal players in the drama personally, and had all been "connected" for some lengthy period of time with the Shiite movement in the Middle East.

Let me put it, at least for reporters and editors, in an even more familiar way. Many of the biggest breaking stories in recent years have been in the developing world: the Iranian hostage crisis, the bombing of the Marine barracks in Lebanon, the dramatic change of government in the Philippines, and the turmoil in Central America. I became convinced many years ago that prior acquaintance with developing country issues—not to mention knowledge of the tastes and smells in those lands—is indispensable to covering the news these days. It simply isn't possible to catch up with the events by quickly reading official reports and calling government officials—not that one shouldn't use every resource available.

There is absolutely no question that American understanding of the Third World needs to be improved and that American reporting on this collection of sometimes very different countries leaves a great deal to be desired. There is also no question that much of that improvement in understanding and reporting can and must take place in American communities. For while there is no substitute for foreign correspondents, there is also no substitute for the powerful impression the local angle makes in revealing the impact of foreign relations. And that is the message of this book.

Stories within these covers make it clear that American political, social, and economic connections to the developing world are growing by leaps and bounds. Although most Americans do not realize it, we already do about as much trade with the Third World as with Western Europe and Japan combined. And most Americans are only peripherally aware of the extent to which immigration to our shores is driven by political and social upheavals in developing countries.

An underlying message in this volume is that the challenge for Americans is not only to compete for new markets emerging in the developing world but also to win the hearts and minds of Third World peoples, even if we never meet them personally. "How is it," a great many Americans ask, "that a nation with such high ideals, such an instinct for benevolence, and such an inbred passion for democracy can be so misunderstood in so many corners of the globe?" It is because we so rarely have any full understanding of the impact we have on other people's lives. How we behave as a nation *does* make a difference, politically and socially.

Some of my colleagues thought it a useless exercise when a friend of mine wrote a book a few years ago on how to behave with the people in Saudi Arabia. Yet the book sold like hotcakes to those businessmen and journalists who knew, at the height of Saudi economic power, that the slightest edge would make them more welcome and thus more competitive in Saudi Arabia.

Think of how much better prepared those of us were who "could see it coming" in Iran or Lebanon, the Philippines, and Nicaragua. And how sweet it is to have been the one who told the home office that there was trouble ahead in Nigeria or Ghana, no quick victory to be won for the Iraqis, or a debt crisis looming in Latin America. I cannot stress the sheer joy and excitement of connecting where others cannot.

And that, as I said, is where this book comes in. It is a simple axiom of journalism that the most effective way to connect with your audience is to make your reporting relevant to an individual's daily life. Along with a number of other experiments, less ambitious but also conscientious, *Main Street America and the Third World* shows that American communities, no matter where they are located, have strong ties to the developing world—ties that reveal themselves in the most vivid and comprehensible ways. This is something I know from personal experience. Not long ago, in Wichita, Kan., I enjoyed the very best Lebanese dinner I have ever had outside the Middle East. I got a lot of useful ''foreign'' information, including that sense of taste I mentioned earlier.

The model stories in this book—gathered on Main Street from Beaverton, Ore., to Winter Haven, Fla.—examine not only the food connection but 22 other Third World ties as well. Each link commands local attention. Just look at some of the headlines that appeared over the stories when they ran originally in hometown newspapers:

WORLD UNREST HITS HOME
FOR LOCAL INDUSTRY

*The* (Aurora, Ill.) *Beacon-News*

TEXAS TOWN FEELS TUG
OF FOREIGN AFFAIRS

*The Dallas Morning News*

AREA CHURCHES GENEROUS
IN THIRD WORLD DONATIONS

The *Hattiesburg* (Miss.) *American*

LOCAL ENTREPRENEURS TAP
INTO GLOBAL TERRITORY:
MISSION OF MARKETING

*The* (Everett, Wash.) *Herald*

## THE COUNTRY DOCTOR:
## THE THIRD WORLD
## CHANGES THE IMAGE

*The Hopewell News*

This last story in a small Virginia newspaper tells how Third World doctors have come to the community and today hold almost half of the physician jobs at the local hospital.

In other words, the story isn't always several thousand miles away. It is at home. This book offers a marvelous way to open that local window on the world.

# Contents

# Acknowledgments

THIS BOOK STARTED as a volume for journalists. It has turned out to be a book for all Americans interested in tracing their connections to the developing world. Not surprisingly for such a work, many hands have shaped it.

To begin with, this book is part of a project under the auspices of the Sigma Delta Chi Foundation, an affiliate of the Society of Professional Journalists, Sigma Delta Chi. The project owes an enormous debt to the three members of the project committee: Alf Goodykoontz, executive editor of the *Richmond Times-Dispatch* and *The Richmond News Leader*; William F. Schmick III, Washington bureau chief for the Ottaway Newspapers group; and Frank Sutherland, managing editor of the *Hattiesburg American* in Mississippi. Russell Tornabene, the society's executive officer, and the rest of the headquarters staff provided support. In particular, I want to thank Grace Roberts for expertly and good-naturedly managing the project's finances, and Ron Dorfman, former editor of *The Quill*, for giving an early boost to this project.

The Ford Foundation, the Carnegie Corporation, and the Benton Foundation funded this project. I am particularly indebted to Avery Russell at Carnegie, without whose enterprise this project would never have been conceived, and to Carolyn Sachs at Benton and Gary Sick at Ford, who have been a consistent source of encouragement and assistance.

Proving that large institutions can be creative, the World Bank gave me the freedom to start this project and, once it was off the ground, a leave of absence to devote full time to it. My work benefited initially from the ideas of Thomas Blinkhorn; I'm also indebted to Dinesh Bahl, José Botafogo Gonçalves, James K. Feather, and Frank Vogl.

The Medill School of Journalism experimented with adapting reporting techniques in this book to the classroom. I am particularly grateful to Dean Edward Bassett, Pat Thompson, Lou Prato, and Charles Alexander, who is also a member of the project's board of advisors and a constant source of sage advice.

Other members of the advisory board are Jo Moring, vice president, Affiliate News Services, NBC News; Patricia Ellis, senior foreign affairs reporter, the MacNeil/Lehrer NewsHour; David D. Newsom, director of the Institute for the Study of Diplomacy at Georgetown University; and Norman Sherman, a writer who defies categorization.

A number of people informally lent their wisdom, talent, and enthusiasm: Carolyn Bantam, Janet Welsh Brown, Milton Benjamin, George Berdes, Jon Blaker, Robert Cahn, Regina N. Hamilton, Beth Hogan, George Krimsky, Don Lesh, Diane Lowrie, Patricia Hill Martin, and John H. Sullivan.

The reporters and media organizations who contributed stories are cited throughout the book. I thank them all for their help and single out several organizations that provided resources that may not be so obvious: the *Hattiesburg American*, a Gannett newspaper, which developed an initial series of stories that gave rise to this project; WSAZ-TV, Huntington, W. Va., a Lee Enterprises station, which under executive editor Bob Brunner produced the television analog of the Hattiesburg series; Media General, which provided substantial support, including funding for the major portion of the poll reported in Appendix Two; NBC News, which produced the pictures that appear in chapter fourteen; and the University of Southern Mississippi—especially Dennis Jones and Susan Siltanen—which contributed expertise in the initial phases of the project.

*The Christian Science Monitor* published eight of the stories in the book on its Business Monday page; there is no more supportive editor than John Yemma, *The Monitor*'s business editor. Thanks are also due to a constellation of other news leaders: Bob

Mong, assistant managing editor, and Cheryl Hall, business editor, *The Dallas Morning News*; Marvin E. Garrette, managing editor of the *Richmond Times-Dispatch*; Kathryn C. Weigel, editor of *The Hopewell News* in Virginia; David B. Offer, managing editor of the *La Crosse* (Wis.) *Tribune*; Georgiana F. Vines, assistant metro editor, and Tom King, assistant managing editor/metro, *The Knoxville News-Sentinel*; Loren Ghiglione, editor and publisher of *The News* in Southbridge, Mass., and the *Bristol Press* in Connecticut, and George Geers, executive editor at *The News*; James H. Ottaway Jr., chairman of the board and chief executive officer of Ottaway Newspapers, and Dave Brace, former managing editor of the *Times Herald-Record* in Middletown, N.Y.; Glenn Gilbert, city editor, and Tal Campbell, managing editor, *The Beacon-News* in Aurora, Ill.

The book is fortunate to have the publishing house of Seven Locks Press with Calvin Kytle, Andrew Rice, and Jane Gold. I was also fortunate to have several able research assistants and graduate students, who dug up the odd fact and brought a good measure of creativity to their assignments: Anne Gibbs, Lucy Alexander, Edward Styck, Nancy Bidlack Simpson, Gina Boubion, Gwen Richards, and David Hosansky.

It may seem improbable that there is anyone else left to mention. The list of people who have helped, however, could be much longer if only to name all of those in towns and cities across the country who agreed to be part of these stories and who proved that Americans are, after all, keenly interested in ways their lives mesh with those abroad.

Finally, it in no way reduces the importance of the above contributions that the final product does not necessarily reflect the views of any of the organizations or individuals who made this project possible.

John Maxwell Hamilton
Washington, D.C.

# Qu'est-ce que
# le tiers monde?

*To talk about the Third World is as descriptive as saying that Korean kimchi and Central American refried beans are, after all, both food. Not surprisingly, countries so labeled don't like the term "Third World," which implies that they hold a lower status than other nations. For the same reason, sensitive people elsewhere use it with some embarrassment, even while realizing that we live in a world marked out by crude categories.*

*The phrase "Third World" is originally French and not pejorative. French intellectual Alfred Sauvy seems to have used le tiers monde first, in L'Observateur in 1952, to describe nations shaking off colonial rule in the same way that commoners—the Third Estate—sought equality with the nobility and clergy during the French Revolution. In the words of French revolutionary Emmanuel-Joseph Sieyès, "What is the Third Estate? Everything. What has it been until now in the political order? Nothing. What is it asking? To become something."*

*In the mid-1950s, many Third World countries tried to distance themselves from superpower confrontation and described themselves as "non-aligned." Today, the idea behind Third World is chiefly one of economic development. Developing or less-developed countries (LDCs) have complicated the issue by organizing themselves into the Group of 77, the Third World economic caucus that really includes more than 100 countries. Development experts, trying to bring more precision to the discussion, have identified a Fourth World, nations with the lowest growth and fewest resources. Throwing up their hands, others simply talk today in terms of North and South, suggesting inaccurately that developing countries lie strictly in tropical regions, while the industrial nations lie in the temperate northern climes.*[1]

*So what is the Third World? It is India with 750 million people and Fiji with 700,000. It is Communist China and conservative Singapore. It is Burkina Faso and Bangladesh, with annual per capita incomes of less than $200, and it is newly industrialized countries (so-called NICs or middle-income countries) like Brazil and Seychelles, with per capita incomes of $2,000. It is oil-rich Saudi Arabia, Venezuela, and Nigeria; and oil-poor Tanzania and South Korea. It is anti-American Cuba and the pro-American Philippines, and it is countries that fight each other, Iran and Iraq. It's also Turkey and Tunisia, Chile and Costa Rica, Sudan and Senegal, Thailand and Taiwan, and Yugoslavia.*

*And it is in flux. White-ruled Rhodesia, some thought, was not in the Third World; its black-ruled successor, Zimbabwe, is.*

Qu'est-ce que le tiers monde? *Too complex for neat definitions. Too big to be ignored.*

---

1. The term "First World" is today used to describe industrialized nations. Eastern bloc countries are sometimes placed in the "Second World."

# Introduction

# Third World News Is Right on Main Street

THERE IS AN unwritten rule among journalists that local news is news and foreign news is foreign, and that people want plenty of the former and will tolerate only small doses of the latter. As a Missouri editor once put it, "The farther it is from Kansas City, the less it is news."

This book challenges that assumption. Events in the poor countries of the developing world—the Third World—definitely do make a difference in Americans' lives. As the stories in this volume show, those events make so much difference that journalists need only look on Main Street America for Third World news—news that will make foreign affairs relevant to the lives of their readers, listeners, and viewers; news that costs no more to cover than a high school basketball game.

## Why Americans need to know

When it comes to identifying the major story of this century, the tendency has been to talk of the rise of American power or the emergence of communism. But the overarching story is more monumental: the emergence of a Third World—more than 100 nations striving for political and economic modernization. The end of the British raj in India and the disintegration of informal Western control over China brought independence to nearly half the people of the world. And to those ranks must be added millions of others in Africa, Asia, and Latin America.[1] Measured by

---

1. As one sign of this trend, the number of nations belonging to the United Nations has increased from its 51 charter members to 159.

their aspirations and their potential to realize them, the development of these nations has significant economic, political, social, cultural, and national security implications for the United States.

Trade offers the most obvious example. From 1970 to 1977, the 20 countries with the fastest growing economies were all in the Third World.[2] Non-OPEC developing countries, which include the poorest Third World nations, increased their share of the world export market by 61 percent between 1970 and 1981. Their share of world imports jumped by even more: 86 percent. At the same time, the American economy has become more exposed to world business trends. Trade accounted for nearly one-quarter of the U.S. gross national product in the peak year of 1981 and is growing faster than GNP. Between 1970 and 1984, for instance, GNP increased 370 percent while trade jumped about 500 percent.

"The level of output and employment in individual countries is now considerably more dependent than it used to be on decisions made by consumers, businesses, or governments in other countries," sums up British economist Michael Stewart. Although it is now more difficult for a single nation to shape its own destiny, interdependence also makes it more important for policy decisions to take global factors into account.[3]

When worrying about war and peace, Americans tend to think in East-West terms. Yet most of the armed conflicts since World War II have erupted in the Third World: South Korea and Vietnam, Afghanistan, Pakistan-India, Lebanon, Iraq-Iran, Nicaragua, Angola-South Africa, and the Horn of Africa. Likewise, U.S. national security depends on sea power, and that sea power depends on the ability to travel sea-lanes and pass through strategic choke points such as the Panama Canal, the straits of Malacca and Hormuz, and the Suez Canal—all bounded by Third World countries.

Seemingly isolated foreign policy objectives or events in the Third World can unravel daily into a tangled set of choices with both economic and national security implications. The U.S.

---

2. John Naisbitt, *Megatrends* (New York: Warner Books, 1984), p. 60.

3. Michael Stewart, *The Age of Interdependence: Economic Policy in a Shrinking World* (Cambridge, Mass.: MIT Press, 1984), p. 22.

government wants military bases in Turkey. Turkey won't agree unless it can export more of its textiles to the United States. Peru says it can't stem the flow of illegal drugs out of its jungles without more foreign aid from the United States. Even a shift in the weather can make a big difference. "It is no accident that in the United States the Central Intelligence Agency was one of the first to try and assess the political and economic implications" of regional climatic change, observes Crispin Tickell.[4]

One need look no further than the news business to see how U.S.-Third World connections crisscross. The Media General newspaper group jointly owns a newsprint mill with the Mexican government in San Luis Potosi, Mexico.[5] When United Press International was about to collapse in 1985, a Mexican publisher stepped in to save it. The Associated Press earns about 3.5 percent of its annual revenue selling services in Third World countries, and it has news exchange arrangements with about 20 developing country press agencies. And where are journalists looking for libel insurance? Bermuda. The Mutual Insurance Company of Bermuda insures more than 700 daily newspapers. With a $10,000-plus annual per capita GNP, Bermuda is not, strictly speaking, a Third World country. But it has yet to achieve a varied, modern economy, and its comparative advantage in insurance is typical of many small developing countries. The Mutual Insurance Company, founded at the request of the American Newspaper Publishers Association, can offer expanded libel coverage "because of its offshore location, which afford[s] substantial tax and regulatory advantages."[6]

*Why Americans don't know*

National agencies and organizations pay close attention to U.S.-Third World relations. The Department of Commerce monitors foreign investment in the United States; the Department

---

4. Crispin Tickell, *Climatic Change and World Affairs* (Lanham, Md.: University Press of America, 1986), p. 1.

5. Although the great majority of U.S. newsprint comes from Canada, suppliers also include developing countries such as Gabon, Saudi Arabia (!), Brunei, and China.

6. Michael Massing, "Libel Insurance: Scrambling for Coverage," *Columbia Journalism Review* (January/February 1986): p. 38.

of Agriculture watches the monsoon in India to forecast levels of U.S. food exports; the American Council of Life Insurance keeps an eye on Third World mortality rates for its members, who sell life insurance policies overseas. In April 1985, the International Brotherhood of Teamsters opened an office in Taiwan, its first in Asia; according to general president Jackie Presser, the Teamsters "will soon have training and information centers throughout East Asia." And developing countries certainly watch us and try to influence policy. "Lobbying for newly industrial countries (NICs) is Washington's latest growth industry," observes Bruce Stokes, international economics reporter for the *National Journal*.

But Americans generally haven't paid much attention to the Third World. For all the cocktail party conversation about "what a small world it has become," most think about interdependence in the same way smokers think about lung cancer. They know the connection exists, but not for them.

There are good reasons for this.

One is that national statistics are abstract. It is one thing for the Treasury Department to estimate that every $1 billion lost in exports puts 25,000 Americans out of work. It is quite another to pick out the 425,000 Americans who became jobless because debt-ridden Latin American countries had to cut imports from the United States by almost 50 percent between 1981 and 1983.

Another reason is rooted in American history. Endowed with a rich continent many days' sail from Europe, not to mention Asia, most Americans have never thought very seriously about foreign trade. Even at the turn of the century, when political leaders began to talk about opening foreign markets, businesses did little to follow. In 1929, a peak business year, total foreign trade accounted for only 12.5 percent of the American GNP, about one-fourth to one-fifth the percentage for the United Kingdom, France, and Japan during the 1920s.[7] With seemingly unlimited national resources, Americans believed they could get by largely without imports.

---

7. Actual percentages are: United Kingdom, 1924-28, 38.1 percent; France, 1919-28, 51.3 percent; and Japan, 1918-27, 35.5 percent. Kuznets, *Modern Economic Growth*, pp. 312-314, as cited in Peter J. Katzenstein, "International Interdependence: Some Long-Term Trends and Recent Changes," *International Organization* 29 (Autumn 1975): p. 1032.

Long-standing cultural ties with the Old World, Europe, also obscure American recognition of the importance of the new, Third World that has emerged. Fledgling and often chaotic governments add to the seeming insignificance and inscrutability of developing countries—never mind that they have much longer histories than we do and richer cultural traditions.

Few Americans—including journalists who are trained to do so—have acquired the habit of asking the right questions. Thinking that no local ties exist to the developing world, they do not look for them. Business leaders in particular are reluctant to volunteer information. They often fear their Third World connections may seem like bad news to fellow citizens in the community. As more than one reporter who worked on the stories in this book has found, workers in plants often don't know their company is investing overseas to take advantage of cheap labor or to gain a foothold in a foreign market.

Ironically, just at the time when interdependence is becoming more acute, journalism trends make it more difficult to improve coverage of foreign events. In 1983, *The Washington Post* figured it cost $130,000 a year to keep a reporter in Harare, Zimbabwe, and $150,000 to keep one in West Africa. Those costs are beyond the scope of all but a few news organizations. Even wealthier ones have cut back. In part, this reflects another trend—emphasis on local news. The United States' largest media group, Gannett, stresses this approach. Its national newspaper, *USA Today*, assiduously hones local angles. Gannett relies on wire service reports, stringers, and occasional staff reporting trips for its foreign news. It has no full-time foreign correspondents of its own.

*A solution on Main Street*

This book advances a solution to these problems. The stories that follow prove that Third World news exists right on Main Street. Each story, written in a different locale, illustrates a different connection with the developing world.[8] Because this book is meant to serve as a resource for those who want to examine

---

8. The stories in this book have been edited for style and space considerations according to *The Associated Press Stylebook*; footnotes have been prepared according to *The Chicago Manual of Style*.

their community's ties to the developing world, each story has an introduction putting it in a larger context and suggesting related themes. A list of sources in Appendix One (with mailing addresses and telephone numbers) identifies national organizations that can provide general background information, as well as local and regional authorities. The people quoted in the stories suggest good hometown sources. Many journalists will find they already have these names in their Rolodex but have not used them as sources for information on the wider world. For as surely as communities have Third World connections, they have people who can talk about them.

Business executives can talk about the complex process of economic development abroad. Consider these two events in East Asia, both gleaned from conversations with local business executives:

—In an interview at the newly built Leaf River Forest Products plant in New Augusta, Miss., corporate executives explained why they decided to target the Indonesia market for their pulp. That country had just passed a new literacy law—which meant it would need more books... which meant it would need more paper... which meant it would need more pulp.

—In another interview, the president of an industrial printing equipment manufacturer in Keene, N.H., was enthusiastic about news of a new Malaysian consumer protection law. The measure required that food processing companies put dates on their products. The New Hampshire businessman saw a new market for his printing equipment.

Several national publications can help identify local businesses involved in international trade. Two of the best are *Thomas Register of American Manufacturers* and *Exporters Directory/U.S. Buying Guide*. State directories often exist. Many federal agencies with international agendas have regional and state representation; for instance, the Commerce Department's Foreign & Commercial Service has offices in 70 cities. At the state and local levels, government agencies have begun to work at increasing exports and enticing foreign investment into their area. Among the best sources on local smaller businesses are community bankers because they help hometown firms arrange exports and imports.

Agricultural extension agents are often knowledgeable on the world food market. In preparing the first stories developed in this project, the *Hattiesburg American* in Mississippi found one of its best sources on farm issues in Malcolm Broome, an agricultural agent working for the county. He could explain what products were exported and how they were shipped. If anyone had called him when President Nixon imposed a moratorium on soybean exports in 1973, Broome would have commented on the local implications. The moratorium, he knew, would increase domestic supplies and thus lower prices for American consumers. It would also force foreign customers to turn to other international suppliers, like Brazil, and thus make it more difficult for Mississippi soybean farmers to export their soybeans later.

Like universities across the country, the University of Southern Mississippi in Hattiesburg has experts on a wide range of international issues. One political science professor, James Wolfe, is active in mediation efforts between Turks and Greeks in Cyprus. On one occasion, the president of the Turkish administration in Cyprus sent Wolfe a letter rebutting issues raised by his Greek counterparts, with whom the Turkish leadership does not speak. Realizing the letter was an important step in negotiations between the two sides, Wolfe forwarded it to the Greek leaders. Odd as it may sound, Wolfe said later, "At one point, the channel of communications between the two governments in Cyprus was through Hattiesburg."

Once reporters start looking and asking the right questions, the list of local experts seems unlimited: church leaders, former Peace Corps volunteers, travel agents. In Hattiesburg, even the local barbershop turned out to have experts. When I stopped in one day to get a haircut, the barber told me he had just returned from two years in Fiji, where he taught barbering. The woman next to him had grown up in Asia, where her father worked for an oil company; another woman was from Central America.

*How to read this book*

There is no single right way to read this book. Some may want to read it all the way through because of its general interest. Others may skim or skip around, looking for stories and sources

7

that apply most readily to their community. Whatever approach, readers—especially reporters and editors—should keep several things in mind.

—Just because it doesn't seem at first that a story idea will work, don't rule it out. Almost every story in this book applies to any community. To prove that, no attempt was made to choose ideal localities for stories. In a couple of cases, it turned out that Third World connections were decreasing or not important. But even that is newsworthy. The best example of this is the story on foreign investment in Dallas (chapter eight). In the late 1970s, people worried that the OPEC dollars would take control of the local economy. It didn't happen—and in 1986 the people of Dallas wished Third World investment would increase and revive the sluggish real estate economy.

—Don't assume that only large daily newspapers can use these techniques. The newspapers that worked on the stories in this volume range from *The Hopewell* (Va.) *News*, circulation 7,000, to *The Dallas Morning News*, circulation 360,000. A twice-weekly newspaper, *The Holton Recorder* in Kansas, used the techniques, as did two nearby high school newspapers. The approach also works for the electronic media. Bob Brunner, executive editor at WSAZ-TV, an NBC affiliate in Huntington, W. Va., proved that. One of his stories has been adapted for this book.[9] And a magazine, *New England Monthly*, prepared a long article looking at interdependence for one community, Westfield, Mass.—once the world's principal manufacturer of buggy whips.

—It doesn't require a seasoned foreign correspondent or international economist to tackle these stories. Young journalists in their first reporting jobs wrote some of the stories in this book. Some of the best ideas for stories came from students at Northwestern University, which experimented with these techniques in the classroom during the 1985-86 school year. As A. J. Liebling once put it, "A good reporter, if he chooses the right approach, can understand a cat or an Arab."

In fact, you don't have to be a journalist. Students in any number of disciplines, members of civic associations, and

---

9. A complete set of WSAZ-TV tapes are on file at the Society of Professional Journalists.

members of religious groups can piece their world together following the story ideas here.

—Don't think of these stories simply as a one-time series of features. An initial series is an excellent way for reporters to educate themselves and their readers on the range of connections that exist with developing countries. But once that foundation is laid, journalists can incorporate Third World angles into their regular reporting. When writing a routine September story on enrollment at the local university, a reporter should ask if the numbers of foreign students are up or down. When interviewing the new president of the largest local business, ask how he views export possibilities. After dedicating one issue of the Wooster, Ohio, *Daily Record* to local Third World news, publisher Victor Dix decided to run additional stories from time to time using the same logo, a series of flags surrounding the words "An International Community." Many pieces in this book coincided with ongoing news events; many were written under normal deadline pressures.

—Get below the surface. Try to use the stories as a window on foreign events. Ask why Third World student enrollment has changed. Is it up for students from countries with booming economies? Is it down for those whose governments have balance-of-payments problems?

For a better sense of the big picture, try the library. Almost 1,400 libraries serve as repositories for federal reports and congressional hearings. The World Bank in Washington, D.C., publishes up-to-date statistics on developing countries, ranging from their debt to the number of doctors they have per capita. The State Department publishes a series of briefs on individual countries called "Background Notes" and policy summaries called "gist." The International Trade Commission produces reports on specific industries. Several reference books found in libraries can also help. The *Oxford Economic Atlas of the World* and the *Encyclopedia of the Third World* contain good general information on trade and other data.

—Finally, these Main Street approaches are useful in looking at industrialized countries or at the Soviet Union—although those nations are relatively better covered than most developing countries.

*Who cares?*

Don't fool yourself that nobody in your community really cares about his foreign ties. Appendix Two summarizes the results of two polls conducted in connection with stories run in the *Hattiesburg American* and the *Richmond Times-Dispatch*. In brief, these "before and after" surveys showed not only that Americans will read Third World stories and want more of them but also that their views on interdependence change as a result of such reporting.

The anecdotal evidence is equally as persuasive. After the *Hattiesburg American* ran its Third World series, the editor estimated the paper received five times the calls it normally gets for its hottest stories. The day after the *Times-Dispatch* ran stories on local economic connections, the local Rotary Club invited the two reporters to give luncheon speeches. In researching stories, reporters typically found that local folks enjoyed helping. Rita Giordano of the Middletown, N.Y., *Times Herald-Record* said that after her series on immigrants appeared, interviewees called "to talk almost like you were a friend."

*The long term*

Readers should be forewarned about the tenor of the stories in this book. Even in the best of times, of course, Third World-related news is not always good news. But recently the news has been notably bad. Third World indebtedness, commodity prices at their lowest point in 50 years, drought in Africa, and adverse weather elsewhere have combined to thwart economic growth in poor countries. United States policies have exacerbated the inevitable repercussions. In the area of trade, the easiest to measure, the strong dollar relative to other currencies has priced U.S. exports out of some markets. The American predilection for using economic sanctions to penalize other nations has worked against overseas market development, whatever the merits for foreign policy might be. Economists, business executives, and political leaders have poignantly argued that decreased flows of new commercial bank lending have held back the Third World's economic recovery. Not surprisingly, this bad news has surfaced repeatedly on Main Street America and in this book.

Had these pieces been written five years ago, they would have been more upbeat. And the next five years will probably be brighter. Starting from a low economic and education base and having little modern experience at self-government, Third World countries have great room for growth. And they have shown that growth is possible. Although they still have a long way to go before their social statistics are on a par with those of industrialized nations, developing countries as a whole saw their citizens' average life expectancy increase from 44 years in 1960 to 59 years in the early 1980s. The adult literacy rate was up 43 percent. A premise of this book is that current economic troubles are temporary setbacks and that economic and social advances will continue.

As a book of news stories, this volume does not volunteer strategies or new public policies relating to the Third World. Nevertheless, it should convey one fact: that Americans cannot choose to isolate themselves from the rest of the world. And the book does suggest questions that deserve wider debate: What can be done to ensure that developing countries achieve economic and political stability; what are the best policies for promoting trade; what should be done to retrain U.S. workers who lose their jobs because of Third World imports; what are the pluses and minuses of protectionism; how adequate are our laws relating to transnational information flows; has the U.S. devoted sufficient attention to becoming a "fast follower," able to copy others' technological breakthroughs as well as to pioneer innovations; what are the real goals of foreign aid and the benefits of economic development abroad?

The central question for journalists is whether they will put such questions on the public's agenda. The techniques outlined here are not the only ways to increase American understanding. Indeed, journalists need to improve traditional approaches, including the fielding of more foreign correspondents. Whatever steps are taken, though, Americans must understand that, today, foreign news *is* local news. Otherwise, they will miss the biggest story of this century and the next.

# 1

# Manufacturing Trade: The Two-Way Street

*THE YEAR IS 1963.* David F. Putnam, president of Markham Machine Co. in Keene, N.H., foresees "a vast [international] market available to firms which will investigate the potential." Five years ago, Putnam himself began to look toward Europe for markets to sell his printing machines. Since then, the company's trade with those countries has increased from 5 percent of total business to 25 percent; it now has British and Dutch sales offices. Putnam expects international trade to account for half his business in the years just ahead, reports the *Keene Evening Sentinel* in its series, "Foreign Trade: How It Affects New Hampshire."[1]

*The year is 1986.* "I see the Third World as a major, major market opportunity during the next ten years," says Putnam's son, Thomas, now president of Markham Machine. Markham, which has "Corp." in its name today, already sells in developing countries such as Mexico and Bangladesh. Tom Putnam has plans for joint ventures in Brazil, Singapore, China, and Australia. As predicted, half the company's business is overseas. Putnam's goal is to increase that proportion to two-thirds. That only makes sense, he says. Two-thirds of the world's gross national product lies outside the United States, and Markham intends to keep up with trends.

Markham's growth mirrors changes in American manufacturing. When it was founded in 1911 by Thomas Putnam's great-grandfather, Markham manufactured equipment to print sizes on

---

1. Today the paper is called *The Keene Sentinel*; publisher James D. Ewing wrote the series.

shoes made locally. Nobody makes shoes in Keene today. Markham has survived by responding to domestic technological changes, making machines to print wattage on light bulbs and codes on integrated circuits, and by adjusting to foreign markets. When shoe production moved to Europe, Markham followed. It shifted again when the Third World began to make shoes. As a result, Markham's work force in Keene has more than doubled since 1963 to 700, and the company has nearly as many people working in facilities abroad.

The story of Keene's rapidly shifting economy is repeated across the United States, but often with little understanding of the forces at work. The local angle is typically one of "winners and losers," with the accent on those at home who have been hurt, observes *Richmond Times-Dispatch* managing editor Marvin Garrette. Journalists, he argues, need to look at all sides of the trade issue. He gave that assignment to three members of his staff, who produced the stories in this chapter.

Special assignments editor John Dillon, who directed the project, started by identifying two specific industries, one that benefited from trade and one that suffered. Then two reporters, Richard E. Gordon and Keith C. Epstein, interviewed executives and workers in local plants. For general information on overall trade patterns, they talked to local bankers and Commerce Department officials. Richmond Red Cross volunteer Liane Egan, a native Brazilian, translated overseas telephone call interviews. Both stories appeared on November 24, 1985, under the title, "The Third World Comes Home."

# Exports Mean More Jobs For Richmond

RICHMOND, Va.—Mike Dance, who never understood why he had to suffer through two years of high school Spanish, was a little surprised to find himself cutting sheet metal for machinery bound for Argentina, Taiwan, and the Philippines.

"I always wondered in school why you had to have a foreign language. Now I see we do deal with foreign goods," said Dance, a spark plug of a man who works at Cardwell Machine Co. in Chesterfield County. "Salesmen, foreign languages, overseas—now I understand."

Cardwell Machine makes products for the tobacco industry. U.S. firms buy most of them, but with only slow growth in that industry in this country, Cardwell executives see Third World markets as a key to the company's future.

"The market for new machinery in the United States is not as great as it once was. To make up, you've got to look beyond our shores," Charles A. Hotchkiss, its president said.

In the Richmond area, long a center of the U.S. tobacco industry, more than a dozen companies make or distribute tobacco machinery. For several, there is no choice but to export, and the Third World's economies are the most promising markets.

In Indonesia, for example, cigarette sales are increasing by 9 percent a year, said Eldon D. Gooden, president of MacTavish Machine Manufacturing Co. In the United States, because of health concerns and higher taxes, sales have been gradually declining.

For American industry, the need to export extends far beyond companies making tobacco machinery.

"As the U.S. economy matures, exports are becoming more important," said Dr. John Parkany, a business administration professor at the College of William and Mary.

"Since our economic growth has slowed, we cannot

realistically expect that our manufacturing will grow except through exports.''

Virginia's chemical, cigarette, electric and electronic equipment, and food are among U.S. enterprises that have developed export markets. Machinery and high-technology equipment also are particularly strong export products to less-developed countries, which want to build up industries to employ their workers and improve their balance of trade, Parkany said.

Mike Dance and other Virginians know from personal experience that exports mean jobs—their jobs.

In 1983, when the Third World economy slumped, Cardwell had to trim its work force. Until Cardwell's business picked up, Dance was out of work.

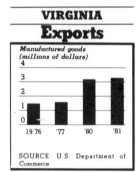

### VIRGINIA
### Exports

Manufactured goods
(millions of dollars)

SOURCE: U.S. Department of Commerce

### VIRGINIA
### Jobs

Manufacturing jobs due to exports (in thousands)

SOURCE: U.S. Department of Commerce

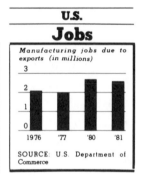

### U.S.
### Jobs

Manufacturing jobs due to exports (in millions)

SOURCE: U.S. Department of Commerce

## TOBACCO PROCESSING MACHINERY
## Export Destinations

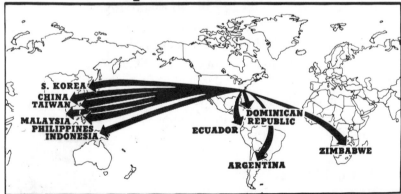

John T. Ailor, *Richmond Times-Dispatch*

Kenny Johnson, 26, of Richmond recently left his job at the Newport Shipbuilding and Dry Dock Co. for a position as a welder for MacTavish Machine Co. on Hermitage Road in Henrico County. Johnson was working last month on a conditioning cylinder, a typical export item used in processing tobacco leaves for cigarettes.

On the other side of the James River, in Chesterfield, Lee Hall and David Satterwhite were checking a melange of sprockets, blades, and belts on a machine that cuts the tips off tobacco leaves. The men, employees of Newcomb's Enterprise Inc., were rebuilding the machine for shipment to an R. J. Reynolds Industries Inc. factory in Ecuador.

There are 200 workers at Newcomb's, MacTavish, and Cardwell alone. There are hundreds more at other tobacco machinery businesses in the Richmond area. Executives of the three companies said exports, mostly to Third World nations, have represented from 5 percent to 50 percent of their business in recent years.

Statewide, as of 1981, there were 46,000 people making manufactured products or materials for export, according to the Department of Commerce. One of nine Virginians working in manufacturing owed that job to exports.

In the Richmond area in 1981, 4,800 people—one of every 11 working in manufacturing—were involved in making products for export, according to computations Parkany made using Commerce Department figures.

With $3.3 billion worth of manufactured exports in 1981, Virginia ranked 16th among the states. Growth in exports generated about one-fourth of the increase in the state's manufacturing production between 1977 and 1981, according to the Commerce Department.

In general, he said, U.S. companies have been slow to promote exports, mostly because the domestic market is so large. For the better part of two centuries, that was largely true of the tobacco industry.

But after World War II, cigarette manufacturers changed that pattern.

The "American blend" of cigarettes caught on overseas in

the 1940s and 1950s, largely because GIs smoked them while stationed abroad. U.S. companies began setting up foreign subsidiaries, and many Third World countries began growing tobacco themselves.

Brazil, one of those Third World countries that has begun to compete for international markets, has become the second largest tobacco exporter after the United States, and its export business is growing rapidly.

The United States imports almost 500 million pounds of tobacco a year, two pounds for every citizen, but exports slightly more. It sends enough cigarettes overseas each year to give 15 to every person on the planet.

In the tobacco business, there are two broad categories of machinery. One is used in processing: cutting the stem off the leaf, chopping the leaf into pieces, and treating the resulting product so it is usable in cigarettes.

Processing machines include threshers, which cut leaves; separators, which divide the leaves and the stems; cylinders for moistening and conditioning; and a variety of equipment to blend, sort, and transport tobacco.

In the other category are the cigarette-making machines, which are highly complex devices that can make as many as 150 per second. Though American companies, particularly AMF Inc., once dominated this business, today a handful of European firms lead the industry.

In the view of some analysts, AMF and other U.S. firms forfeited the cigarette-making machinery market to the Europeans by not developing advanced equipment. A 1983 International Trade Commission report quoted unnamed industry sources as saying that government-sponsored anti-smoking campaigns led American manufacturers not to invest in research and development.

For the processing machines, though, an international market has developed because of the increase in tobacco cultivation abroad, particularly in the Third World.

Ironically, the popularity of the high-speed European machines among U.S. cigarette makers has led to higher demand for U.S.-made processing machinery. That is because only the new American machinery chops leaves into pieces large enough for the new cigarette machines to use.

Cardwell, which traces its roots to 1829, has long been an international leader in tobacco-processing machinery. U.S. firms, including Cardwell, MacTavish, and Newcomb's, still dominate the trade in these machines.

Some of the exported machines are purchased by American companies, such as the Richmond-based Universal Leaf Tobacco Co. and Dibrell Brothers Inc. of Danville, which have extensive overseas tobacco-processing operations. The machines are also purchased abroad by government cigarette monopolies, private businesses, and subsidiaries of American cigarette companies.

Processing machines built in Richmond can be found in Indonesia, the Philippines, Argentina, Thailand, China, South Korea, Malaysia, Thailand, Zimbabwe, Ecuador, and the Dominican Republic.

Export sales of these machines grew steadily through the late 1970s and early 1980s, peaking in 1981, according to Commerce Department statistics. For Cardwell, 1981 was a record year, with $11 million in sales, including $7 million in exports. Hotchkiss, Cardwell's president, said most of the machines went to Third World countries.

With the export market booming, Cardwell had increased its work force to 190, almost twice as many people as it has today. Then the market dried up. Reasons included a general recession and developing countries' severe foreign debt problems, which caused governments to restrict imports, Hotchkiss said.

Suddenly, recalled Dance, 31, who came to the plant in 1975 as an apprentice sheet metal mechanic, "it seemed like the foreign market came to a halt."

"When I was laid off, I knew that it had to happen. It was more important for the company to survive than for me to have a job. The worst that could have happened was for the company to fold."

Cardwell was never in danger of closing, Hotchkiss said. But it had to trim its sails, and today, with Third World economic problems persisting, it makes $6.5 million worth of equipment a year. (A London-based subsidiary, which serves the European and African markets, has comparable annual sales.)

"Latin America has completely dried up because of the debt problems the countries have," Hotchkiss said. "But certainly Asia is a viable market. We think it's coming back."

Hotchkiss and Ed Ward, international sales manager for Cardwell, have traveled extensively in the Far East. Ward was based in Manila for more than eight years as a one-man foreign office.

"The key thing I learned when I worked there was patience," Ward said. "You have to forget Western mentality and think along the lines they think."

Parkany and other experts agree that American firms must persevere.

"Almost every industry has a significant export activity," Parkany said. "But they haven't achieved their potential."

—**Richard E. Gordon**
*Richmond Times-Dispatch*
November 24, 1985

# Imports Posing Threats to Jobs In Blackstone

BLACKSTONE, Va.—You can see the world in a pair of shoes.

Consider the shoes on your feet. They could very well be made of American leather that was tanned in Japan, South Korea, or Taiwan; assembled with low-cost labor; then shipped to the store where you bought them.

Or consider the shoes in the front window of the Peebles store at Main and Elm in Blackstone. On the soles are the words, "Made in Brazil."

Just down the road is the factory that shut down last year because of these shoes. A slick "for sale" sign reads "Available." It might also be a statement for many of the 250 people who used to work there.

One of them, Virginia Lewis, was nearly 55 when the plant closed. Hoping to open an antique shop, she had poured any extra money from her wages into a saving account. This month, she withdrew the last $27 from that account.

The account was at a Virginia bank, of course. As it happens, Virginia banks are among the many U.S. financial institutions that have lent funds to Brazil, money used in part to build the factories that made the shoes that helped put Virginia Lewis out of work.

The development of national industries has been good for Brazilians. Shoe factory wages are still lower than those in any other major shoe exporting country, and their standard of living isn't on a par even with poor Americans, but they've come a long way.

Paulo Strecker, 37, is especially fortunate. He is a supervisor at one of the 4,000 mostly new factories in the state of Rio Grande do Sul and, as such, has been able to buy a dishwasher and washing

21

machine for his wife, who used to do that work by hand.

It might have been Paulo Strecker's plant that made the shoes at the corner of Main and Elm.

For Virginians this tie to the developing world is one of personal and community setbacks, and of recriminations.

—The factory workers, mostly women with family ties that keep them in some of Virginia's poorest areas, blame imports and the state's largest shoe company, Craddock-Terry, which closed two plants late last year.

—The communities in which those plants were fixtures, Dillwyn and Blackstone, also point their fingers at Craddock-Terry, which they courted with financial enticements less than two decades ago. Each spent tens of thousands of dollars, public and private, to buy land, make improvements, and offer other incentives to build the factories.

Dillwyn town councilman Maynard Davis, one of 20 businessmen who put up money to buy land for the factory, says he'd never do it again. "Why stick your neck out and get walked on?"

—Critics of the industry, among them U.S. retailers who have prospered and gained jobs in the boom of foreign-made shoes, say U.S. shoemakers like Craddock-Terry were inefficient and shortsighted and failed to spot fashion trends. In short, they did themselves in.

"They're wedded to certain types of shoes," argues Peter T. Mangione, president of Footwear Retailers of America.

Some critics say U.S. companies shouldn't be in the shoe business in the first place: Labor costs too much.

And some local critics accuse Craddock-Terry. Luther P. Gilliam, a former superintendent at Dillwyn, claims the firm discouraged faster, better-paid workers and failed to correct inefficiencies by cross-training workers. The company responds that while "no plant in the world is 100 percent efficient," Craddock-Terry's was as good as any.

—Then there's the company itself. Craddock-Terry's chief executive officer, G. Bruce Miller, blames President Reagan for failing to provide protection earlier in this year, and he bitterly calls the ITC—which in June had urged Reagan to restrict imports—"a joke," "a waste of time."

—Fingers are also pointed at three countries that constitute nearly three-fourths of the foreign competition: South Korea, Taiwan, and Brazil.

—And Brazil points the finger back, saying that the only way it can hope to develop or repay its $105 billion debt is by exporting—particularly shoes, which has grown into its No. 1 industry.

"It's not just important that we sell shoes to the United States—but essential," says Brazilian Embassy spokesman Antonia Gonçalves. "If we don't export, we can't pay off this debt."

Bitterness and blame are not unique to shoe imports.

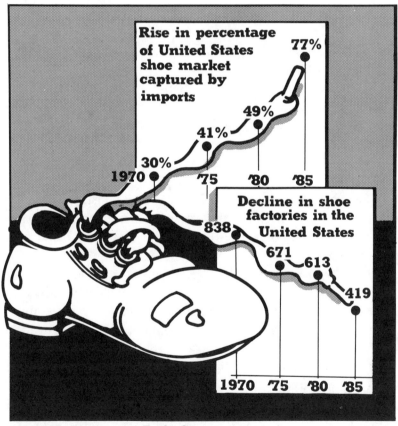

**Rise in percentage of United States shoe market captured by imports**

77%
49%
41%
30%
1970 '75 '80 '85

**Decline in shoe factories in the United States**

838
671 613
419
1970 '75 '80 '85

SOURCE: International Trade Commission
John T. Ailor, *Richmond Times-Dispatch*

There is so much fervor to curb imports these days that in Congress more than 400 bills aim at cutting foreign competition on everything from automobiles to water bed mattresses.

On November 14, the Senate approved legislation to force cuts in textile, clothing, shoe, and luggage imports. It's likely to be vetoed by Reagan, whose administration favors free trade and is wary of foreign regulation.

The government says that 1.7 million U.S. manufacturing jobs have been lost since 1979, many because of imports, and ahead looms a $150 billion trade deficit.

At Blackstone, the end came in late October 1984 in the person of Roland K. Peters, a Craddock-Terry vice president, who doesn't like to talk about how bad he felt the day he told 250 people they were out of work.

The workers were told to shut down their machines and gather near the door of the packing department. There they found Peters, standing on a table.

To the workers, his face was familiar. During that last year of falling profits, faltering production, and shortened workweeks, Peters twice had to come to lecture on imports. "This is our competition," he would say, holding up samples of Brazilian or Taiwanese imports. "We've got to be efficient. Look what we're up against."

It is what the entire shoe industry is up against: lower wages and lower prices. Shoemakers argue that since foreign workers earn less, foreign companies can sell for less—and capture the market.

A shoe worker in Blackstone, for instance, paid on average $4.50 an hour, earned more than twice as much as a Taiwanese and more than five times as much as a Brazilian. The woman's casual shoe produced at Blackstone could be made in Taiwan for one-fourth the cost.

The bottom line: Three of every four shoes sold in the United States are imports.

As a result, the U.S. footwear industry claims it has lost 20,000 jobs and, since 1970, 419 factories—one of every two.

The Blackstone plant was typical. Opened amid optimism in 1970, it could have churned out 3,600 pairs a day. It never did.

Instead, orders dwindled, and by the end of 1983, it was limping along at 24 percent of capacity.

For the entire year, despite significant losses, Miller ordered Dillwyn and Blackstone kept open. He was hoping for import relief.

It never came. "We gambled and we lost," he recalls.

The shoe industry as a whole gambled $1 million to mount the campaign to limit imports. The ITC was sympathetic, but Reagan, the son of a shoe salesman, argued that with import quotas American consumers would pay $3 billion in higher shoe prices.

In the end, the shoe industry found itself up against the most fundamental notion in American business: Enterprise should be free of government interference; the fittest should survive.

It's also a fact that many shoe companies have compromised their anti-import stand to save themselves.

When sales of Dillwyn-made shoes faltered, Miller imported uppers from Brazil. This year, at least $7 million—one-tenth of Craddock-Terry's sales—will come from shoes imported by the firm from Brazil, Taiwan, South Korea, Italy, and Hong Kong. Now Miller is negotiating with the Japanese and may open a shoe plant there.

Today, one-third of all foreign-made shoes sold in the United States are imported by U.S. manufacturers. At least 12 have affiliates in foreign countries, from Haiti to Malaysia.

In Blackstone that October day, it fell on Peters—a soft-spoken, friendly man thought of more as an uncle than as a vice president—to deliver the bad news.

"I'm sorry," he began. "As you all know, imports have gone up. Our shoes are not moving. Believe me, we kept you as busy as we could."

"I cried," recalls Mrs. Lewis. "I felt like the bottom had just fallen out. I kept thinking: What does a 55-year-old woman do when there are no jobs? I mean, with a husband who's disabled, where do I go from here?"

For many others, economic troubles compounded other setbacks. Shortly after Gale Legassey lost her job in a shoe factory, her husband became too ill to work. Several years earlier one of her two daughters had died.

"All we ever wanted to do was make a decent living and provide for our children," Mrs. Legassey says. "But now I can't even buy her a decent pair of shoes."

Wilma Rutledge, a mother of two, also lost her job when the shoe plant closed. She now commutes 42 miles a day to learn new skills, those of a secretary. She faces the prospect of getting a job in Richmond, a 60-mile trip each way, but at least it's a prospect.

Meanwhile, shoe exports have provided hope for many Brazilians. The state of Rio Grande do Sul, where Paulo Strecker works, had only 125 shoe factories 15 years ago. Today there are 4,000.

Banks and major department stores have moved into towns. Shoe workers still earn low wages and have poor, cramped housing by U.S. standards. But, says Rogerio Dreher, executive director of the Association of Footwear Industries in Rio Grande do Sul, "things are so much better. So many people find the quality of life improved."

Maintaining shoe exports—$835 million worth last year alone—is critical for Brazil, which has the world's largest foreign debt. Brazilian officials say that 50 cents of every dollar earned in exports goes to pay back U.S. lenders.

Bank of Virginia is one of those lenders. At $35 million, its loan is a drop in Brazil's debt bucket. But assuming Brazil makes its payments, the bank will earn $700,000 per year on the 12-year loan, which means shareholders will get their share of more than one-seventh of that, a bank officer estimates.

Bank of Virginia's loans to Brazil have been for commercial and governmental development.

"Normally, I'd be sympathetic to the local customers losing their jobs," says the bank's senior vice president, Leslie P. Hunter. "But that's taking a purely provincial view. You've got to take a global view."

—**Keith C. Epstein**
*Richmond Times-Dispatch*
November 24, 1985

# 2

# Third World Imports: Good Business

JOBLESSNESS created by Third World imports is one side of the story. Another side is how imports save money for consumers, put people to work, and ensure that U.S. exporters continue to have markets.

Imported shoes do well in the United States because they carry lower price tags. The *Richmond Times-Dispatch* article in chapter one noted the projected cost of shoe import quotas to American consumers: $3 billion. Estimates generally show that this greatly exceeds the amount earned by workers whose jobs are saved.

Moreover, for many Americans, imports mean jobs. In an effort to stay competitive at home and abroad, American businesses have begun to use imports themselves. Foreign imports account for more than 40 percent of the American bicycle market. The Schwinn Bicycle Co., once a strictly domestic company, now imports 60 percent of its products from Japan and Taiwan.[1] Numerous small American businesses import materials like steel or small pieces of equipment like motors, which they can often get more cheaply *and* more quickly from Brazil and other developing nations.

Moreover, imports create work for trucking and rail companies, customhouse brokers, international trade attorneys, and ports. Imports have transformed New Haven, Bridgeport, and New London—all in Connecticut—into booming ports. "Even though it's bad that people lost their jobs in Youngstown to a mill

---

1. Keith E. Leighty, Associated Press story in *The Washington Post*, July 7, 1985.

in Brazil, the availability of high-quality, inexpensive steel keeps jobs in Connecticut,'' says one port operator.[2] Says a banker in Virginia, where imports have put shoe workers out of jobs, ''There are a lot of people who put food on the table and shoes on the kids because Mother Nature gave us one of the world's best natural ports'': Hampton Roads.

Finally, there is concern that steps to stop imports will spawn a worldwide wave of protectionism that would hurt American exporters. ''Imports are so integrated into the fabric of U.S. society that protectionism may be shooting ourselves in the foot,'' says Adrian T. Dillon, an economist with Eaton Corp.[3]

In 1986, *The Knoxville News-Sentinel* decided to go beyond the typical imports-equal-joblessness stories. Business editor Jane Gibbs DuBose started by looking at the *Directory of Tennessee Manufacturers* to identify likely companies, and she then conducted a series of interviews with their executives and workers and with local retailers and economists. Her five stories, two of which ran on the front page, looked at local ''buy-America'' campaigns, technological advances to produce goods more cheaply, and import and marketing strategies to remain competitive with Third World countries. One of those pieces appears below.

*Tulsa Tribune* reporter Mike Ward wrote the second story reprinted below. His report examines the pluses and minuses of imports and protectionism from the vantage point of a clothing store on Main Street in Stillwater, Okla. In addition to local interviews, he called the Mauritian Embassy and the State Department in Washington, D.C.

---

2. Quoted by Mark Potts, *The Washington Post*, December 20, 1984.

3. Quoted by Dale D. Buss and Paul Ingrassia, *The Wall Street Journal*, October 28, 1985.

# Knoxville Beats Competition By Joining It

KNOXVILLE, Tenn.—Knoxville Glove Co. has operated for decades on the banks of the Tennessee River. It plans to stay. But a map of its future has roads leading to the Orient.

Like other manufacturing companies, Knoxville Glove faces tough competition from Third World exports. To cope, the company will focus on two survival strategies—becoming an importer and securing orders for specialty gloves—said President Rodman Townsend Jr.

As an importer, Knoxville Glove would put its name on gloves made overseas, then distribute them to its customers in the United States.

Other East Tennessee producers also say importing gives them flexibility to weather economic swings, to supply buyers who want a full line of products, and to provide steady employment to their hometown work force with less possibility of layoffs.

Townsend believes manufacturers in China, Hong Kong, South Korea, and Taiwan are about to take over the U.S. market for standard-made cloth gloves. Leather gloves made overseas have more than 80 percent of the market now, and fabric gloves, 55 percent, Townsend said.

If those percentages grow, domestic producers will be forced to concentrate on synthetic gloves and on specialty gloves for workers in heavy industry or for the military.

Townsend plans to contract with a glove-making plant in the Orient for the first time this fall. Currently, the company is buying gloves made overseas from a "middleman."

"One goal we have is to provide whatever a company needs for a line of goods," he said. "Imports are already dominant, and I would expect they are going to be even more so."

Knoxville Glove isn't the only company to take a deep breath and play the Third World survival game.

Armstrong Rubber Co.'s tire plant in Clinton, 20 miles north of Knoxville, does business with Taiwan's third largest tire maker, Hwa Fong. The Far Eastern firm makes tires for golf carts, lawn mowers, and boat trailers using Armstrong's specifications and bearing Armstrong's name.

"We use them to supplement our capacity, and they use us as a marketing arm," said Ed Morris, general manager of the plant.

"It's mutually beneficial. It's also our insurance policy. We make it ourselves and it keeps the foreign suppliers out of our customers' offices."

Morris said it's difficult to find an American plant capable of producing tires for Armstrong because the number of domestic small-tire makers has dwindled to three.

"We have nowhere to turn in the United States."

Armstrong also is more comfortable setting up a business relationship with a company abroad than revealing trade secrets with a domestic producer who is more of a competitor, Morris said.

Hwa Fong makes less than 10 percent of Armstrong's small tires. Overall, the plant manufactures 11,000 to 12,000 small- and industrial-sized tires a day.

Golf carts and boat trailers are primarily products for Americans; therefore, the market has little chance of expanding.

Tires on golf carts don't have the reputation for quality to maintain that tires on passenger cars do, Morris said. Foreign producers can offer tires to cart makers confident consumers won't notice they aren't American-made, he said.

"People are price buyers. To the uninitiated, a tire is a tire. Who cares? It's round and it's black."

For these reasons and because of the enormous cost of setting up a new plant, Armstrong feels comfortable as an importer.

If an order for thousands of tires were canceled, Morris would cut back production in Taiwan rather than in Clinton, where 285 people work as salaried "associates." He would be able to continue to supply his clients.

Importing also keeps capital investment at a minimum. Armstrong Co. plans to spend some $10 million on new equipment in Clinton. Investing millions more for a new building and more equipment to accommodate periods of overcapacity isn't feasible, Morris said.

"We have very little investment in it except the inventory," he said.

Bike Athletic Co., which makes athletic gear and apparel, is also operating at capacity at its Knoxville plant.

Last year, it struck a deal to transport cut material to an operation in Juarez, Mexico, where it is sewn and brought back to the United States. A few months ago, Bike Athletic started a similar venture in Kingston, Jamaica.

In both countries, workers earn from 25 to 30 cents an hour, compared to the average $7-an-hour wage for the 700 Bike Athletic workers.

Jim Corbett, Bike Athletic president, isn't bothered that athletes across the country could be wearing football pants made in Third World countries.

"We're contractors. It's no different for us than if we were contracting domestically, but it happens to be more economical," Corbett said. "It helps us level our work force."

Shipping precut material to Caribbean countries is gaining in popularity among apparel makers, who can take advantage of geographic proximity to buyers as well as tariffs that are lower than if they imported a fully made garment.

Duty is paid only on the value-added portion of the commodity, and that value is modest because of the low-cost foreign labor used in the sewing operation.

"We keep our factories full," Corbett said of Bike, whose owner is Colgate-Palmolive Co. "We only take excess capacities to this type of operations."

The 807 operations, so named because of the section of the U.S. tariff code that allows lower duty, give Bike the chance to do what its competitors are already doing, Corbett said.

Apparel imports have grabbed up to 45 percent of the U.S. market and could have 80 percent by 1990, according to Data Resources Inc., an economic consulting firm.

Producers in the Far East are also in demand from companies

such as Standard Knitting Mills of Knoxville for sportswear.

Standard, whose parent company is Stanwood Corp. of Charlotte, N.C., buys 2 to 3 percent of its total output from a Hong Kong company that makes shorts, shirts, and slacks bearing Standard's Pony brand name.

Standard has been able to protect most of its business by relying on products such as underwear and fleece wear that require a minimum of labor.

Executives admit manufacturing abroad is a double-edged sword that could wound them unless they continue to find ways of staying ahead of Third World competitors.

"It depends on how much of the marketplace we are willing to give them," Morris said.

—**Jane Gibbs DuBose**
*The Knoxville News-Sentinel*
March 30, 1986

# Local Families Coming To Rely On Imports

STILLWATER, Okla.—Sam Bates was stumped when the big cardboard boxes arrived at his Main Street clothing store last summer. The stylish, plaid sports shirts inside looked 100 percent American but bore an unfamiliar foreign label:

Made in Mauritius.

"No one was sure where that was, so we looked it up in the atlas," explained Bates, a clothier here for 40 years.

"Mauritius is in the Indian Ocean someplace. We got a geography lesson with the shirts."

The shirts—sewn on the archipelago where the flightless Dodo bird became extinct 250 years ago—now are a staple item on shelves in Stillwater and across Oklahoma.

The distance between Bates' cash register and the tropical island plant where the shirts were made demonstrates the ticklish balance that has come about with growing U.S.-Third World trade.

On one side are U.S. manufacturers, who are demanding strict import quotas to guard against the erosion of more American jobs to foreign competition.

Import quotas could limit the number of shirts Bates could buy from Mauritius.

On the other side, economists and trade experts contend that protectionism—import quotas—will drive up prices in the United States.

And, they warn, U.S. protectionism could result in other countries limiting their purchases of U.S. goods, such as soybeans and wheat grown by Stillwater farmers.

"International trade must be fair—both ways," replies U.S. Rep. Wes Watkins, whose 3rd District includes Stillwater.

"Import restrictions may cause some reprisals. But to do nothing will only erode our manufacturing base even more, and endanger national security."

Bates' shirts are only one of dozens of imports that fill Main Street stores, including shoes from Brazil, rattan furniture from Taipei, Romanian glassware and wood carvings from Kenya, dolls from Guatemala, and scarves from Afghanistan.

The same is true in other cities and towns across Oklahoma.

"American consumers have come to rely on imports, whether they realize it or not," Bates said. "The biggest reason is the price."

If the $35 plaid shirts had been made in the United States, they would cost $5 to $10 more.

"The labor costs are so much less overseas that they can sell for less, even with the additional transportation costs," he said. "Ten years ago, a lot of these items were made in the United States. Now they are coming in from the Far East and Europe.

"Americans have priced themselves out of the market with high labor costs."

That change has made Mauritius, Thailand, Malaysia, Taiwan, Macao, China, and Sri Lanka into major clothing supply centers alongside Hong Kong and Singapore.

Bates said the result has doubled the lead time for ordering apparel, but consumers have benefited at the cash register.

"Some Far Eastern goods used to have workmanship problems, but those have been corrected. American companies supply American patterns and provide American supervisors," he said.

"Most people like the style and the price, so they buy. Only a few older customers look to see where it was made."

In contrast, October [1985] surveys by Gallup and Roper found that if the price and quality are identical, Americans prefer to buy U.S.-made clothing.

Marketed under the Izod Lacoste label, Mauritian shirts are manufactured in a plant outside the capital of Port Louis. Shipped by air to New York, they arrive in Stillwater by truck.

The plant is among several developed to bolster the island's sagging economy, wracked by chronically high unemployment, a 1980 cyclone, and low world prices for its chief export, sugar.

About the size of Rhode Island, Mauritius is a former British protectorate located east of Madagascar and populated by about 950,000 people of Creole, French, English, Hindu, and African descent.

Most exports from the French-speaking island have traditionally gone to Europe. Commerce Department figures show U.S.-bound exports—mostly clothing and knitwear—have increased in the past three years.

P. F. Fulena, first secretary of the Mauritian Embassy in Washington, said uncertainty over the transfer of Hong Kong from British to Chinese control at the end of the century has also shifted some plants to the island.

World Bank reports show Mauritius has an international debt of $208.9 million and relies on sales such as sports shirts in Stillwater to keep its overseas loans paid.

Unemployment and a militant opposition have plagued the parliamentary nation, which gained independence from Britain in 1968.

A cutback in exports because of U.S. trade quotas will cost Mauritians jobs and could destabilize the economy, Fulena said.

"We expect to develop more trade with the United States,

not less," he said. "We have no trade restrictions. Free trade is much better."

At home, Congress has more than 300 bills pending to restrict trade, ranging from strict quotas on single imports to sweeping surcharges on all imports.

Commerce Department reports show special trade restrictions now cover 21 percent of all imported goods, up 8 percent from 1975.

In a recent report, the International Business and Economic Research Corp. estimated that domestic apparel producers would gain 71,000 jobs if Congress passed the pending textile imports bill.

Retailers, however, would lose 62,000 jobs.

Although there would be a net gain of 9,000 jobs, the study calculated that it would cost $369,000 per job saved—or a total of $3.3 billion.

According to a state Department of Economic Development report, 1,278 people lost jobs with the closing of 20 Oklahoma clothing plants between 1982 and 1984.

Those are among a total 526 plants that closed in Oklahoma for all reasons during the same period and cost 11,869 jobs.

Commerce Department figures show an estimated 3.4 million Americans' jobs depend on imports.

In short, if imports such as the shirts are stopped or cut back, fewer U.S. workers will be needed to haul, unload, and sell the goods.

Fewer workers will mean fewer service-related jobs.

Another 5.4 million Americans owe their jobs to the $204 billion in goods and services the United States exports annually.

U.S. Sen. Don Nickles, R-Okla., warned that the pending trade protectionist measures could cost agriculture $12 billion.

"There's no sense in cutting off our nose to spite their face," Nickles said. "Agriculture is our nation's only export industry with a positive trade balance. But it won't stay that way if the protectionists damage our export markets."

Nickles estimated that 6,000 Oklahoma farm jobs could be lost if import restrictions—such as clothing quotas—are approved.

Foreign governments whose U.S. markets are cut off will

retaliate by canceling wheat, soybean, and cotton purchases.

A Federal Reserve study in November concluded that protectionism in three industries—clothing, autos, and sugar—cost U.S. consumers between $14 and $19.5 million in 1984.

"Protectionism breeds higher prices," said Phillip Willis, a Commerce Department trade analyst.

"The imports cost more because there are fewer of them. And domestic goods cost more because there is less foreign competition."

Watkins, a member of the Democratic Task Force on Trade, argues that other factors must also be considered. He views protectionism as a way of reversing the trade deficit, which reached $150 billion last year.

"The trade deficit is a threat to national security," Watkins said.

Others argue that the United States will come out ahead only if it lowers the strong dollar and if its businesses take steps to be competitive.

Bates sees little future in protectionism. His shelves hold sweaters made from Uruguayan wool, umbrellas from Taiwan, tweed jackets from Scotland, wallets from Spain, and rainwear from England—to him, symbols of inevitable global trade.

Even if protectionist legislation blocks imports from some other countries, Bates said, "the American environment is so competitive that other suppliers would probably replace the present ones.

"Somebody would find some other country with cheap labor costs and would start making [clothing] there.

"If people want something, the free enterprise system will probably supply it."

—**Mike Ward**
*The Tulsa Tribune*
March 24, 1986

# 3

# Third World Imports Keep U.S. Industries Humming

"WHEN OUR FOREFATHERS founded this country..., the United States had an abundance of raw materials like lumber, iron ore, and coal. At the time, we enjoyed the isolation of two oceans and did not have to compete with the rest of the world for markets or raw materials," said H. Eugene Frymoyer, vice president of purchasing for Carpenter Technology Corp. "However, the Lord put space-age materials in strange places, and this country is highly dependent upon imports to satisfy many of our metal requirements."[1]

Americans have traditionally viewed developing countries as sources of relatively insignificant commodities. But the banana republic image no longer fits.

To start with, food imports include much more than bananas. Thanks to modern transportation and climatic differences, developing countries give us not only coffee, tea, and cocoa, but also a wide range of fresh fruit and vegetables in the winter. The United States, the world's largest food exporter, is also the world's second largest food importer.

In addition, developing countries, particularly in Southeast Asia, supply us with the hardwoods we use to make furniture. They send 100 percent of our natural rubber, most of which is used in tires; diamonds and fertilizer; and, of course, oil. Mexico supplies 100 percent of American strontium, a mineral used in television screens to block X-rays. Hercules Inc., a chemical

---

1. Speech at Kutztown University of Pennsylvania, March 7, 1984.

company, imports an estimated two million tons of rosin every month, mostly from China. Hercules uses rosin to make adhesives, inks, and about 1,000 other products, which it often exports to developing countries.

Third World nations have also exported ideas for using raw materials. In 1983, the Conference Board, a New York business and economic research group, conducted a survey of technology imports by U.S. manufacturing companies. Business executives reported looking to countries such as Indonesia for advanced thin wood veneer technology, Brazil and China for metal castings technology, and Romania for advanced mining equipment and transportation technology.

One journalist has commented that any newspaper can put together a story on raw materials simply by sending out a questionnaire to local businesses, asking what they use and where they get it. Numerous small- and medium-sized towns have businesses that deal with strategic minerals, which go through a number of processing steps before ending up in a finished product. Consider the travels of rutile ore, imported from Sierre Leone, among other places. A Gulf & Western plant in Ashtabula, Ohio, converts the ore into titanium tetrachloride. OREMET Titanium in Albany, Ore., turns the chemical into titanium sponge. RMI Co. in Niles, Ohio, takes the next step of producing titanium ingots that can be fabricated into specialized shapes by Advanced Alloys Inc. of Hauppage, N.Y., or Cucamonga, Calif. Finally, defense industries use the titanium in aircraft, satellites, helicopters, and missiles.

One of those defense-related manufacturers is TRW Inc., the subject of the story below.

# Ohio Brings African Alloys To U.S. Defense

CLEVELAND—The machine operator watches the freshly made automobile valve rumble into position. With the press of a button, sparks fly; he puts a cobalt alloy coating on the part, which topples into a box.

The roar of metal on metal in this TRW Inc. plant in suburban Cleveland is a sound straight out of mid-America's manufacturing region. But the cobalt, more often than not, is from Zaire and other developing countries.

Although Americans think of their country as a land of abundance, Third World raw materials keep U.S. industries humming. Many of those industries are critical to national security.

The United States simply does not have domestic reserves of some minerals. Limited domestic mining of cobalt, among many other minerals, is possible, says Timothy Stanley, chairman of the International Economic Policy Association, but "the costs would be prohibitive."

The need to maintain reliable supplies of raw materials has forced businesses and political leaders to become more sensitive to Third World developments, particularly since the Soviet Union is the key alternative supplier for many minerals.

The United States imports over 90 percent of its cobalt, tantalum, chromium, columbium, and platinum-group metals, says Arden L. Bement Jr., one of several senior executives at TRW's corporate headquarters in Lyndhurst, Ohio, who closely follow raw material imports.

TRW's sprawling family of manufacturing facilities makes wide use of these five minerals in superalloys: Tool plants in Rogers, Ark., and Augusta, Ga., use tantalum and columbium; a third in Boone, N.C., uses platinum-group metals to make electric resistors.

39

Just down the road from here, in Euclid, TRW uses chromium to produce control rod drives for nuclear reactors in submarines and jet engine turbine blades. Altogether, the F-100 jet engine in the F-15 and F-16 fighters uses 1,485 pounds of chromium.

Superalloys, capable of performing at high temperatures, are made up of a large number of imported raw materials. Stellite—the cobalt superalloy used here to extend the wear of valves—consists of chromium, nickel, and tungsten, among other imports.

A TRW risk analysis showed that in 1980 the corporation imported critical materials from 27 countries, 21 of which are Third World nations ranging from Argentina to Zimbabwe.

"We sit squarely in the middle of the production pipeline," says George A. Harris, TRW vice president. With no large-scale mining or processing operations of its own and no retail selling of raw materials, he says, TRW's position "is the same as that occupied by a large number of businesses—small as well as large—in the United States."

Cobalt mined in the southern African country of Zaire reaches TRW through a long process complicated by all the intricacies of international politics and economics. Zaire ships cobalt ore and refined powder via its own West African port or through white-ruled South Africa, Marxist Mozambique, or socialist Tanzania.

Secondary producers in the United States import the cobalt. They refine it to achieve greater purity or to make stellite and other superalloys, which TRW buys.

In an earlier era, large mining companies could operate relatively freely throughout a region or even globally. American corporations, Harris says, "relied on their suppliers' strategies" for acquiring materials.

Today it is not so simple.

Raw material commodities are the only major source of export earnings for many developing countries, whose young economies have not yet achieved significant industrialization. Intent on gaining control of these resources, just as they gained political independence, they have nationalized mining operations and sought better prices.

Zaire, which accounts for well over half of all cobalt production in the Free World, has suffered debilitating economic set-

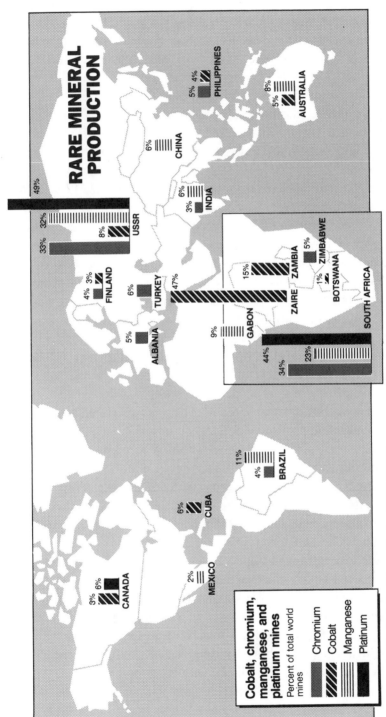

RARE MINERAL PRODUCTION

**Cobalt, chromium, manganese, and platinum mines**

Percent of total world mines

- Chromium
- Cobalt
- Manganese
- Platinum

CANADA 3% 6%
MEXICO 2%
CUBA 6%
BRAZIL 11% 4%
USSR 49% 32% 8% 33%
FINLAND 4% 3%
ALBANIA 5%
TURKEY 6%
CHINA 6%
INDIA 6% 3%
PHILIPPINES 5% 4%
AUSTRALIA 8% 5%
ZAIRE 15%
ZAMBIA 5%
ZIMBABWE
BOTSWANA 1%
GABON 9%
SOUTH AFRICA 47% 44% 23% 34%

Joan Forbes in *The Christian Science Monitor* ©1986 TCSPS

backs since independence in 1960, in part because of its own mismanagement of resources. But thanks to recent economic reforms, Zaire has "integrated its industry much faster than anyone expected," Bement says. U.S. government analysts believe it has used its commanding position to boost worldwide prices, which sagged during the global recession.

In the United States, Zaire now works through a single distributor, Afrimet Indussa Inc., in which it has a financial interest.

These changes strengthening Zaire are good for U.S. industry, some observers say. They ensure a more reliable supply of cobalt.

A wide range of foreign policy issues complicates mineral imports for Americans. The United States imposed an embargo in the 1970s on chromium imports from Rhodesia (now Zimbabwe) as part of its strategy to press the white government into accommodating the country's black majority. American business had to import from the Soviet Union, which accounts for nearly one-third of the world's chromium production.

The Soviets also produce about one-third of the world's manganese and nearly half of the platinum metals.

South Africa is especially well endowed with mineral resources. But industry executives say its apartheid policies make it a candidate for an American embargo.

Internal political turmoil common to many newly independent countries can threaten supplies. Rebel disruptions in Zaire during 1978 caused cobalt prices to quadruple temporarily.

American industries have met this complex world by paying more attention to Third World issues and maintaining lines of communication with the developing nations. Corning Glass, which needs superalloys in high-temperature production processes, has conducted an annual raw materials assessment for six years and sends representatives to southern Africa regularly, according to David Anderson, its manager of raw materials purchases.

When TRW faced the possibility in 1978 that Zairian cobalt might not be available to its American producers, the corporation took the unusual step of buying cobalt itself.

It has also tried to stay in step with Third World development strategies. Thailand plans to use more of its tungsten and tin in manufacturing, and to cut imports of finished products. Taking advantage of this, TRW is entering into a joint venture with the Thais to make engine valves.

The need to ensure adequate supplies of minerals in the event of a U.S. national emergency has sparked heated controversy over the Strategic Materials Stockpile. Levels in the federally run stockpile are supposed to be sufficient for military and essential civilian needs during a three-year conventional war.

But in recent years levels have chronically fallen below goals, in large part, critics say, because successive administrations have sold off stockpile resources to help balance the budget.

A group of outside advisors to the Interior Department has recommended setting up a separate government corporation that would shield the stockpile. A bill in Congress would set stockpile levels by law.

Although TRW executives support reforms, they do not see the stockpile by itself as adequate even for national security. "You need shockload protection," Harris argues. "It is not a long-term solution to anything."

In a recent report, the Center for Defense Information in Washington, D.C., criticized one solution: a buildup of Navy forces to protect sea-lanes through which mineral imports would flow. That, it said, would increase the risks of military involvement when other steps would be more effective.

Among the suggestions the center and others offer are to use foreign aid programs to build up mineral production in countries that are not currently exporters, to engage in more vigorous government research for mineral substitutes, and to barter.

Under the barter program, which was used extensively before 1973, the United States traded surplus food for foreign minerals. The only recent deal involved an exchange of dairy products for Jamaican bauxite.

Diversifying production of cobalt requires rises in depressed prices for copper and nickel, according to the Bureau of Mines. Copper and nickel are mined with cobalt.

New Caledonia, the Philippines, Finland, and Botswana started cobalt mining operations in 1960. Additional production may be possible in the Southwest Pacific.

Tax incentives and relaxation of pollution standards, Bement says, would encourage "some [American] industries on the ragged edge of being profitable" to go back into production.

TRW is also searching for mineral substitutes. Amid the din in this plant, TRW has put up a quiet laboratory for development of ceramic engine components. Norton Laboratories is helping.

TRW's need for materials may diminish slightly if it is able to sell the jet engine facility in Euclid, part of its strategy for streamlining the corporation.

But no alternative strategy will ever eliminate the need for imports, Harris says. And whoever buys the jet engine plant will also buy a relationship with the developing world.

**—John Maxwell Hamilton**
*The Christian Science Monitor*
March 10, 1986

# 4

# Learning To Live With Third World Markets

DOING BUSINESS in Third World countries offers financial rewards, as the foregoing stories tell. For many companies it will mean the difference between growth and no growth, perhaps even decline. But it also adds a new dimension of challenge and risk.

As our economy becomes more interdependent with other nations, so does it feel the impact of Third World events. History, unfortunately, has poorly prepared Americans to cope with a complex, interconnected world. The United States has never been a trading nation like Britain or the Netherlands, and many U.S. businesses are uneasy about breaking tradition. Linda M. Daniels, a reporter with *The News* in Southbridge, Mass., found that most businesses in her community simply don't want to get involved with trade at all.

The difficulties of learning to work in foreign cultures is a story by itself, one that any business executive who has worked internationally can relate vividly. Anyone exporting chicken to the Middle East must arrange for special slaughtering procedures required by Moslems. Pizza Huts offers fish toppings in Asia. In the 1970s, when Boeing wanted to develop Third World markets, it modified its 737s so they could tolerate bumpy runways. (Sales soared.) The DHL courier service, with offices in more than 40 African countries, must charter a special plane to retrieve packages from cities close to the war zone in Angola. It has an experienced courier aboard the ferryboat between Kinshasa, Zaire, and Brazzaville, Congo, to overcome bureaucratic hurdles. In Latin America the Campbell Soup Co. puts its product in bigger cans because families south of the border tend to be larger. Chevrolet Nova had a major problem in Latin America: In Spanish, *no va* means "no go."[1]

Journalists do their community a major service by explaining how small and mid-sized companies can get into the exporting business and who in the community and state can help. Linda Daniels' articles on trade, prepared for *The News'* "Annual Business Review and Forecast Supplement," extensively quoted local citizens who knew the importance of foreign commerce. Of developing countries' economic potential, one local business leader said, "The thing American companies have to keep in mind is that these countries develop slowly, but when you invest in them you invest in the future."

The piece below looks at the impact of Third World mishaps on business in the Fox River Valley in northern Illinois. The story is by R. C. Saponar, a business reporter with *The Beacon-News* in Aurora. Perhaps the most remarkable aspect of her report is that, troubles notwithstanding, businesses in the community are not nostalgic for the days when Americans did not think about world markets. They look ahead to competing for a bigger share of foreign commerce.

---

1. For other examples, see Carole Sugarman, *The Washington Post*, November 11, 1984; Kenneth Labich, "America's International Winners," *Fortune*, April 14, 1986; Howard Schissel, *Journal of Commerce*, May 14, 1986.

**46**

# Third World Problems Hit Fox Valley

AURORA, Ill.—In 1979, the fundamentalist government that had just taken power in Iran informed Barber-Greene that it was withholding payment on $11 million worth of machinery ordered by the previous regime.

Last month they paid.

The six-year-long episode, involving complex trading arrangements that were finally settled by an international claims tribunal, illustrates the unpredictable pitfalls that trouble companies in the Fox Valley who have increasingly looked overseas for new markets.

"The difficulty here was we didn't provide for revolution," said Frank Merrill, president of Barber-Greene Overseas Inc. The firm is a subsidiary of Barber-Greene Co., an Aurora-based manufacturer of specialized road construction equipment.

"You have to be careful with overseas business because you can't put all your eggs in one basket. It could all end with one gunshot," said Larry Harms, director of international operations at Aurora Pump. The North Aurora manufacturer of centrifugal and turbine pumps is a unit of General Signal.

The problems of becoming heavily involved in exporting have emerged clearly during the past several years.

Developing countries' growing debts, the strong dollar, more foreign competition, and depressed worldwide markets have combined to put a dent in U.S. exports.

As countries such as Argentina and Peru have piled up more debt, they've been forced to reduce shopping lists that include U.S. goods. Simultaneously, the strong dollar has hindered U.S. sales abroad, making American products more costly.

Companies that have come to depend on export markets have been especially hurt. Caterpillar Tractor Co.'s overseas business has dropped by 13 percent compared to a decade ago. This is critical because a large share of Cat's total sales—42 percent—is still exported or manufactured abroad.

Annual exports for the manufacturer of earth-moving and construction equipment plummeted from $3.5 billion in 1981 to $1.8 billion last year.

The work force at Cat, one of the top 10 U.S. exporters, doesn't resemble its former self. The number of U.S. workers making Cat's exports has been slashed in half since 1980—from 31,000 to 16,000.

During the same period, the number of workers at Cat's plant south of Aurora in Montgomery dropped from 6,350 to 3,225.

"It shows what depressed markets overseas will do to you," said Don Defoe, Cat's governmental affairs representative for international issues. "We had to scale back on production—in the United States and abroad."

Barber-Greene exported 70 percent of its U.S. production in the late 1970s, according to Merrill. Today, exports have dropped to between 10 percent and 15 percent of a much reduced total.

Closure of Barber-Greene's manufacturing plants in Aurora and Elgin earlier this year were just part of the company's three-year plan to return to profitability.

"There's always been somewhere in the world going up and another going down," said Merrill. "But three years ago we caught them all going down and it was disastrous."

One former major market for U.S. products that has dried up is the Middle Eastern oil-producing countries. OPEC countries had been a prime market in the 1970s when oil was in demand and profits overflowed.

"The Middle Eastern countries were good markets for Cat," Defoe said. "When those countries were cash rich, they were doing a great deal of development."

Oil exports have been on the decline since the late 1970s, however, leaving less money for road improvements and related purchases. Many development needs just aren't being met since bills can't be paid.

"We think *we've* got potholes. *They've* got potholes we could

*Logos of Fox Valley firms involved in Third World Trade*

lose 100 of our potholes in,'' Merrill said. ''It isn't a question of need; it's a question of money.''

Decreased revenues for developing countries have cut overseas business from 11 percent to 7 percent for Equipto, an Aurora manufacturer of steel shelves, racks, and cabinets. A 4 percent decline in exports can make a big difference, according to Tom Voigt, manager of Equipto's international department.

''In a good year, it's frosting on the cake,'' said Voigt. ''In a poor year, it's the difference between a substantial layoff and a minor layoff.''

Equipto employs about 300 people. For a four-month period in 1983, Voigt said, there were some layoffs while domestic sales were sluggish.

It has become more difficult to arrange sales in many developing countries. U.S. commercial banks are wary of providing letters of credit, or payment guarantees, for export sales to Peru, which has balked at international debt rescheduling proposals.

''It has affected us to the point where we're more cautious in how we sell,'' said Dave Moir, international sales manager for Furnas Electric Co. The Batavia firm manufactures motor controls.

''That's one of our biggest obstacles,'' Moir said. ''We can't get letters of credit confirmed.''

According to Voigt, exports require ''substantially'' more

**49**

paperwork, and the process can get complicated for a novice.

The need for a dozen documents—including letters of credit, bills of lading, certificates of origin, and export declarations—isn't unusual, Voigt said.

"Getting used to the various forms of payment is one of the obstacles, but it can be overcome," he said. "You can still get taken if you're not very careful on how to handle exports and documents."

It's not just complicated paperwork or economic shifts that worry exporters. Cultural misunderstandings—for example, concepts of punctuality and political uncertainties—make foreign markets risky.

The big question in setting up an overseas operation, said Voigt, "is can we recoup our investment before the king is overthrown?"

Some developing countries, particularly those in East Asia, currently provide less risk.

Aurora Pump discarded plans to establish a sales base in Miami for the South American market, Harms said, opting instead for a site in Singapore.

A small assembly and distribution center opening next year in Singapore is being counted on to spur overseas business, he said. Harms predicts the firm's 10 percent annual overseas sales could expand to 25 percent of total business in five years.

Most major U.S. pump companies have a facility in Singapore, according to Harms, where the government offers incentives to foreign business.

Political changes have made India, once highly protectionist, attractive to Barber-Greene. Six months ago Barber-Greene granted a manufacturing license to an Indian company.

"We looked to India for 20 years and never could find our way through that red tape and bureaucracy," Merrill said. "It's vastly different now."

Many developing countries require firms to base operations in their countries if they want to sell domestically. Limited access prompted Barber-Greene to establish a plant in Brazil and prompted Caterpillar to establish one in Mexico.

"In order to supply a broader line of Caterpillar equipment, we determined to have a local presence down there," Defoe said.

Cat's plant in Mexico began production earlier this year. Returns haven't lived up to projections, but Defoe said the Mexican market is expected to play an important future role.

"Estimates for Mexican production are not nearly as great as we once envisioned they would be. . . as a result of international conditions in the country," Defoe said. "We envision that long term, Mexico will be a good market for Cat."

Despite difficulties in dealing abroad, Fox Valley manufacturers agree foreign sales are a vital part of their business.

Furnas Electric, a 25-year veteran exporter, formed an export department in 1978. The company hopes to increase overseas sales, which now represent 2 percent of an annual $85 million sales.

"I think today any company that's in business to stay that doesn't get into foreign business is missing the market. Our company has apparently decided we want to be a factor in the international market," Moir said.

"I think we have to realize the world is getting smaller and we have to get involved in it," added James O'Rourke, executive vice president of sales and marketing for Furnas. "I think we have to consider world markets as we do any other state in the union."

Cat has a 22-point plan to reduce costs by cutting back its production and work force in order to meet lowered demand. Defoe says continuing depressed worldwide markets call for more cutbacks to ensure the company's survival.

"If we're not competitive, there won't be a Caterpillar Tractor to employ people," Defoe said. "We intend to continue as a major exporter. It's going to be difficult, but there's still a substantial number of exports and jobs committed to exports."

**—R. C. Saponar**
*The Beacon-News*
November 17, 1985

# 5

## America's New Farmers' Market

JOE MORGAN, a southern Mississippi farmer, has never tasted soy sauce, a soybean derivative as important to East Asians as ketchup is to Americans. He rarely leaves his Pine Belt, Miss., farm to visit other states and has never traveled to Mexico or Nigeria, where his soybeans are used to make feed for chicken. But he knows that his livelihood is tied to Third World markets.

Every harvest, Morgan hauls his soybeans to the Pascagoula waterfront, where he sells them to the French-owned Louis Dreyfus Corp. Dreyfus loads the produce on vessels bound for Africa, Asia, and every other corner of the world. During the rest of the year, Morgan frequently calls Dreyfus brokers to monitor world grain prices, which he puts on his computer.

The importance of foreign trade for the American farmer is not a new story. Agricultural products made up four-fifths of American exports between 1830 and 1860. Access to overseas markets helped pull America out of depressions in the 19th century and was a central issue in the rise of agrarian revolts. In the wake of the Great Depression of the 1930s, an official with the Agricultural Adjustment Administration commented, "The restoration and improvement of export markets for products of our farms is necessary for the continuance of the existing organization of American agriculture."[1]

So it is today. About two out of every three rows of American

---

1. H. B. Boyd, "Methods of Increasing Agricultural Exports," in *Farmers in a Changing World: Yearbook of Agriculture, 1940* (Washington, D.C.: GPO, 1940), p. 596.

wheat go abroad.[2] Soybeans grown by Joe Morgan and other farmers, along with soybean products, are the United States' largest export by value, bar none. And, as in past eras, farmers continue to fret over the health of foreign markets. The difference is that the markets they worry about are increasingly Third World markets.

With great scope for economic growth and increased consumption, Third World countries have given American farmers vast new export opportunities. Even with increases in their own harvests, Third World countries have difficulty meeting food demand. One reason is rapid population growth. Another is that the poor tend to use new wealth to buy more and better food. Between 1960 and 1980, grain consumption in developing countries doubled. Although their domestic production increased as a result of the "Green Revolution," so did imports. Net imports supplied 4 percent of grain consumption growth in the 1960s and 21 percent in the 1970s.[3]

Even with these gains, scope for future growth in exports remains great. An estimated 300 million to 2½ billion people are still chronically undernourished.[4] Concludes U.S. Department of Agriculture Assistant Secretary Robert Thompson, "The less-developed countries are tomorrow's customers for U.S. farm products, if their incomes can be increased."[5]

If rises in Third World prosperity are good for farmers, declines are bad, as any farmer in the 1980s can attest. Stiff debt-servicing obligations and economic stagnation have forced developing countries in recent years to cut back on U.S. imports. Many of those countries have had to press harder than ever to step up their own agriculture exports in order to earn foreign exchange to pay their debts.

---

2. William E. Kost and Cathy L. Jabara, "Agricultural Trade is Vital," in *U.S. Agriculture in a Global Economy: Yearbook of Agriculture, 1985* (Washington, D.C.: GPO, n.d.), p. 24.

3. Donald O. Mitchell, "Trends in Grain Consumption in the Developing World, 1960-1980," *Finance & Development* 22 (December 1985): p. 12.

4. For discussion of data, see *Ending Hunger: An Idea Whose Time Has Come* (New York: Praeger, 1985), p. 7.

5. Robert L. Thompson, speech at The Agricultural Outlook Conference, Washington, D.C., December 3, 1985.

The story below looks at the farm crisis from the vantage point of farmers in Hunt County, Texas. Finding sources of information in addition to the farmers themselves was no problem. Although the modern farmer may still seem to stand alone in his fields, he relies on platoons of experts: agricultural extension agents, bankers, cooperative managers, economists with the federal government and grain companies, university professors, and port directors. All these people are acutely aware of the importance of exports to the farmer's livelihood—and to their own.

# Farm Recovery Tied to Third World Markets

COMMERCE, Texas—Along the blackdirt fields that fan out from the winding country roads in Hunt County, sweat and good weather once promised farmers a living. Today, prosperity—and, increasingly, failure—depends as much as anything on complex foreign markets, particularly those in poor Third World countries.

"Fun's about gone out of it," says Allen Lynn Martin of Commerce, one of thousands of Texas farmers frustrated by international forces that have spawned a national farm crisis.

With wheat exports expected to decline about 40 percent this year according to USDA estimates, farmers like Martin can't seem to get ahead. Producing bigger harvests—the traditional roll-up-your-sleeves way to earn more—only compounds problems by creating surpluses that drive prices down further.

The current 1.74 billion bushel U.S. wheat surplus is a record level, equal to nearly three-fourths of an average year's harvest. That surplus is largely due to depressed exports, according to the USDA.

Underscoring the importance of foreign markets to farmers, the Reagan administration has built its strategy for solving the farm crisis on expanding overseas sales. Developing export markets is also a key issue in the farm bill debate under way in Congress.

Hunt County agricultural extension agent Bob L. Greenway predicts that current conditions will drive as many as 15 percent of the roughly 250 full-time farmers in the county out of business this year. About 50 farmers have left since the farm crisis began.

The Hunt County experience is being repeated across the country, at all levels of the farm economy. Grain exports leaving the port of Houston, one of the largest agricultural ports in the United States, are down 70 percent so far this year.

"We've been in operation since 1966 here, and we haven't seen anything drop off this quick in 15 to 20 years," says Wayne Slovacek, vice president of Houston port operations for the Union Equity export elevator. "We normally have ships coming in regularly. Now we can go a week without one coming in.

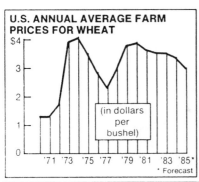

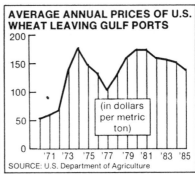

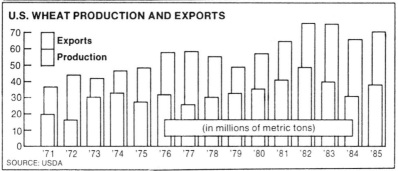

*The Dallas Morning News: Dan Clifford*

"We just can't use what our American farmers are growing," he says.

What makes this state of affairs especially perplexing to veteran farmers like Martin is that it was never supposed to turn out this way.

Foreign markets began to boom in the early 1970s. Big customers such as the Soviet Union and smaller developing nations with growing economies provided American farmers with new, lucrative markets. The switch in 1973 from fixed to floating exchange rates lowered the value of the dollar, making U.S. commodities relatively inexpensive abroad.

Farmers responded by growing record harvests. Overall, agricultural exports jumped from $7.2 billion in 1970 to a peak of $43.6 billion in 1981.

Texas farmland devoted to wheat production more than tripled after 1971. Virtually all of the additional wheat went abroad, according to Bill Nelson, director of the Texas Wheat Producers Board.

By the end of the decade, wheat exports accounted for more than 60 percent of U.S. farm production. The share going to developing countries increased the fastest.

Unfortunately, the situation for American farm exports today, says Mickey Paggi, an economist with the Texas Agricultural Extension Service, "is almost a mirror image of what benefited us in the 1970s."

The value of the dollar is up, 65 percent higher than in 1980, making farm products more expensive abroad. Third World nations once flush with cash have run up large debts. Servicing those obligations has required some countries to cut back imports of even basic foods.

Peru, a Latin American debtor nation, slashed wheat imports nearly in half between 1980 and 1984. Chile's imports are down a third. Ghana's are one-sixth the levels of five years ago.

A number of unpredictable factors have added to farmers' difficulties.

—China's ambitious economic reforms have turned it from the United States' largest importer of wheat during the 1980-81 harvest, when it bought 8.7 metric tons, to fourth this year, when it is buying 2.8 metric tons.

—The embargo on exports to the Soviet Union, after it invaded Afghanistan in 1979, closed a market at a time when other nations were seeking to expand their farm exports.

Among these new competitors are Argentina and the European Economic Community. The EEC's heavily subsidized exports have dominated developing countries in North Africa.

—The sharp rise in oil prices in the 1970s—brought on by petroleum-rich developing nations—raised farmers' costs of doing business. While the price of wheat has declined in absolute and real terms, the diesel that Martin needs to run his tractors has increased eightfold in the last 15 years. Petroleum-based fertilizer has tripled in price.

Heavily in debt themselves as a result of major investments in the growth years of the 1970s, many farmers have tried to cut costs, a trend that is depressing retail farm suppliers' sales.

"This year, sales are down for fertilizer and other products from fencing to animal supplies," says Richard Thomas, manager of the Union Equity Cooperative Elevator in Hunt County.

Adjusting to foreign markets is especially difficult for farmers, who traditionally like to go about their business divorced from the vagaries of the marketplace.

"Typically farmers spend 364 days growing and one day selling," says Greenway, the county's senior extension agent.

Farmers often admit they don't have a solution to the new challenges associated with growing crops for profit in the 1980s.

But, say economists like Carl Anderson with the Texas Agricultural Extension Service, farmers must learn to monitor international prices for their produce, plot selling strategies, and harness their lobbying organizations to press for changes in national macroeconomic policies. For example, the high federal deficit, which many blame for the high value of the dollar, is a major stumbling block to increased exports, Anderson says.

A farmer can independently take steps to reduce his costs and increase yields, says Harry Baumes, an agribusiness economist with Chase Econometrics. When he's seeking to change national policies, "it's best if he can make his voice heard through various farm organizations."

In addition to lobbying Congress and the administration, farm organizations bring in trade delegations and post representatives abroad to develop new markets. The American Soybean Association and U.S. Wheat Associates are encouraging the Chinese to use more of the commodities the United States exports—for instance, soybeans in chicken feed and wheat in Western-style bread.

To maintain and expand foreign markets for their crops, Texas wheat farmers voted this year for a half-cent-per-bushel assessment on wheat to fund marketing efforts of the Texas Wheat Producers Board.

"So far this year, we've collected $600,000, and we've brought seven overseas groups to Texas to show them our ports and elevators, and to keep them interested in buying our wheat," says Nelson of the board. Seventeen other states have similar programs.

The Texas Department of Agriculture, with an eight-person international marketing staff, attempts to match foreign buyers with Texas sellers of crops and livestock products.

In line with its philosophy of upping farm exports, the Reagan administration launched a program to enhance agricultural exports about six months ago. The three-year, $2 billion program challenges export subsidies by other countries with U.S. subsidies.

The initially targeted countries—Egypt, Algeria, North Yemen, and Morocco, who are being given preferential prices on wheat and wheat flour—currently trade with the Europeans.

Last week, the administration initiated international trade dispute procedures against the EEC for unfairly subsidizing its wheat exports.

Farm groups complain that the administration is not doing enough to promote trade and, in fact, has made it more difficult by erecting barriers to manufacturing imports, such as textiles, which encourage protectionism by other countries.

Farmers are also ambivalent about foreign aid efforts that have helped nations increase their own food production and in some cases even become exporters.

"We should be a lot more careful about exporting agricultural technology," says Union Equity's Thomas.

At the same time, farmers recognize that economic growth abroad is essential if purchasing power and imports are to increase in developing countries.

"If the past is any predictor of the future, the newly industrializing countries will be our best markets," says Paggi, especially singling out the developing countries on the Pacific Rim.

Tom Kay, deputy director of USDA's Foreign Agriculture Service, agrees that agricultural export growth lies with those robust economies. Europe is no longer a growth market and neither is Japan, he says. The Soviet Union's plan to achieve food self-sufficiency will make it a less important customer.

For farmers in Hunt County, Texas, the winding roads lead straight to the Third World.

**—Maria Halkias and**
**John Maxwell Hamilton**
*The Dallas Morning News*
October 20, 1985.

# 6

# Hometown Diplomats

CALIFORNIA'S new Export Board announces that it will offer four types of financial aid, including export insurance and loan guarantees, to further overseas sales.

—Illinois opens a trade office in Shenyang, China.

—The lieutenant governor of Delaware, a Chinese-American, tells an American Chamber of Commerce meeting in Hong Kong that his state will soon launch a mission to attract Asian investment into the state.

—Michigan signs a contract with Price Waterhouse to study the possibility of opening an offshore trading company. The most likely spot is in Barbados, says the director of the state's Office of International Development.

These days, when you think about foreign relations, you don't necessarily think about the State Department. You think about the states.

Aware that they must find new ways to revitalize or maintain economic growth, states are doing what was once strictly the province of diplomats and other federal officials. According to a 1985 report issued by the National Governors' Association, 49 states hold export seminars; 30 have some form of overseas representation; and 15 have passed export finance legislation. The average state spends $100,000 a year to woo foreign tourists— and for good reason. Every 55 foreign visitors create one new job in the domestic economy, says the NGA.

Not surprisingly, international trade has become a major state election issue across the country.

And it isn't just the states that are at work. Cities and counties are promoting trade. A 1984 Chamber of Commerce study found that three-fourths of the 84 chambers responding offered programs to help local businesses export. In 1985, 12 small- and medium-sized cities, including Warwick, R. I., and Fort Wayne, Ind., joined together in a Community Development Trading Group. Each member city makes cash contributions and details one city staff member to work with the group.

"It's getting down to where cities are competing with each other for international business," says William Schwartz, former mayor of Wilmington, N.C.

Local efforts to improve foreign relations are not confined to business. Sister Cities International has helped over 750 cities pair themselves with 1,104 cities in 86 countries—for example, Selma, Ala., with Zacapa, Guatemala; Cheyenne, Wyo., with Taichung, Taiwan; and Independence, Mo., with Blantyre, Malawi. The initial contacts are often for cultural exchanges. Sometimes growing ties open a wide array of diplomatic initiatives. As reported by *The Holton Recorder*, a twice-weekly newspaper in Kansas, a one-time president of the Kansas Farm Bureau made four trips to China, first for trade and later to arrange an agreement between Henan province and the state to "share in cultural exchanges, tourism, trade, professional, student and teacher exchanges."[1] Even more political, the Davis (Calif.) City Council endorsed plans for a local group of citizens to make a fact-finding trip to Nicaragua. The state of Maine refused to send its National Guard troops to participate in maneuvers in Honduras when the governor disagreed with Reagan administration policy.

In the story below, which appeared in *The* (Everett) *Herald*, reporter Aly Colón examines commercial diplomacy in Everett, Wash. In putting the piece together, Colón first went to the county Economic Development Council, a membership organization made up of businesses and public officials. The council explained what they were doing to promote trade and investment and gave him a list of businesses involved in overseas transactions. One of those was Royal Dental Manufacturing, mentioned in the lead to the story. The story, said Colón later, prompted a large number of calls to the EDC. Although Royal Dental was on the EDC's list, it hadn't even known the development council could help.

---

1. Lorraine Tudor, a free-lance journalist, wrote the series as part of a local Lenten program series.

# World Trade Now 'Bread and Butter' For Local Business

EVERETT, Wash.—Everybody has teeth. Everybody has problems with them. And the need to treat troubled teeth transcends territorial boundaries.

That line of thinking encouraged Harold Tai, president of Royal Dental Manufacturing located in Snohomish County, to put his money where foreign mouths are—and sell dental chairs in Third World countries.

That same kind of reasoning is also encouraging state and local organizations to help business sell more abroad and to recruit foreign investment.

"The potential is unlimited," said Clare Coxey, president of the Snohomish County Economic Development Council, which wants to help businesses like Royal Dental.

The EDC's emphasis, Coxey said, "is the location of foreign investors in our county for the creation of jobs here."

Coxey has convinced the EDC board and staff to "sell" Snohomish County to Japan and South Korea.

"We've established a sister city relationship with Japan; maybe we should do the same thing with Korea," Coxey said.

The EDC also plans to produce a videotape extolling the benefits of doing business in Snohomish County.

Coxey's approach dovetails with the marketing efforts of the state Department of Trade and Economic Development. Often the EDC and the DTED work together.

Coxey recently traveled to the Pacific Rim with a state investment mission headed by Gov. Booth Gardner.

As Gardner, Coxey, and Tai recognize, the business of marketing one's products no longer stops at local, regional, or even national borders. At least one of every five jobs in the state depends on international trade.

"International trade is the biggest employer in the state," said George Taylor, president of the Washington Council on International Trade. "To Washington, it is our bread and butter."

At a Snohomish-King County Conference on Jobs and Economic Growth last Monday in Everett, John Anderson, DTED's director, devoted his entire speech to the importance of foreign markets to the state's economy.

The state has reorganized the trade and economic development department, increased its staff, expanded its budget, and increased the number of planned trade missions, Anderson said.

The expanded international trade division is looking carefully at Indonesia, Malaysia, Thailand, Singapore, the Philippines, and South America.

The DTED has also created the "Team Washington" concept, which draws the public and private sectors together to work on foreign marketing. The related Washington Ambassadors program trains businessmen for overseas marketing missions sponsored by the state.

Even the changing of the department's name—to include "Trade" instead of "Commerce"—reflects a more aggressive foreign thrust.

Trade is no less important for the county than for the state. The EDC maintains a list of 97 Snohomish County companies that engage in exporting or importing, or both. International trade contributes at least $360 million to the county's economy, according to 1982 figures.

If you throw in Boeing Co. and related aerospace firms, which do substantial foreign trade, that figure balloons up to $2.45 billion, according to a report by the Washington Council on International Trade. That trade activity supports 12,000 jobs.

Many local businesses have acted on their own to develop foreign markets.

Tai at Royal Dental Manufacturing realized that developing countries like Egypt, Colombia, and Venezuela could play a role in extending the life of the dental chairs his company produces.

Dental chairs begin to lose their appeal quickly because U.S. firms want the latest models. Third World countries are not so style conscious.

"Our older products become useful to [firms in developing countries that haven't caught up with the U.S. market]," Tai said.

Other local firms, including Honeywell, Hewlett-Packard, Boeing Co., ELDEC, and the John Fluke Mtg. Co., which are based here or have local subsidiaries, already realize that the lines between domestic and international trade are practically nonexistent.

And with the state's obvious geographic proximity to the developing Pacific Rim, marketing more companies and communities to foreign countries has become an increasingly attractive option for local and state organizations.

On the county level, the EDC counsels companies interested in exporting their products. EDC staff can investigate market potential and provide information on market strategies, agents, distributors, trade shows, patents, and financing.

"We are the linchpin between the clients and the resources they need to market themselves," said Mike Deller, EDC operation's manager and acting director.

Mel Terry, who heads Air Film Corp., a Mountain Terrace-based firm that exports industrial air cushions to northern Europe and South America, believes such assistance can be invaluable.

"Anyone considering [overseas markets] has got to seek professional help," said Terry, who has used trade shows sponsored by the Department of Commerce to help him market his company's products overseas.

Tai's Royal Dental company uses sales representatives and foreign market dealers to promote its products overseas. It has its catalogs at trade shows in Third World countries. The company has also used the U.S. Small Business Administration catalog show program overseas, Tai said.

Soon the EDC hopes to help local firms establish overseas contacts by a computer linkage with the Export Assistance Center of Washington. That will give local companies access to technical how-to information about exporting, Deller said.

The center is a non-profit corporation established by the state to provide export counseling and export loan packaging for Washington firms with annual revenues of less than $100 million.

The EDC also plans to co-sponsor an export-import conference on May 20 and 21. It will be held at the Sea-Tac Red Lion Inn.

Meanwhile, the state is encouraging foreign investors to come to Washington.

"The focus is on the invitation and encouragement of foreign firms to purchase idle businesses or construct new plants," DTED head Anderson said at the Jobs and Economic Growth conference this week.

That investment will lead to new job opportunities, increased economic activity, and a bigger tax base, Anderson said. Although the DTED won't promote specific sites, its efforts through trade missions and contacts with individual companies operating in foreign countries will be the first step to attract investment.

Local communities can follow up through their "Team Washington" connections. Each county, including Snohomish, has its own "team" version that works with the state organization.

In May, for example, members of the state's international trade division of the DTED will go on a mission to Colombia, Ecuador, and Peru. They will take along literature about 20 Washington businesses, involving food processing, storage handling, agricultural, and farm equipment.

"The secret is getting out," Deller said. "People are surprised just how much business we do [overseas]."

—Aly Colón
*The Herald*
March 9, 1986

# 7

# Banking on Development

THE THIRD WORLD debt crisis is a towering example of global interdependence.

The roots of the crisis lie in the steep oil price hikes ordered by petroleum-exporting developing nations in the 1970s. Awash in surplus cash, the newly rich OPEC countries put large deposits in private commercial banks in industrialized countries. The commercial banks, needing to put those petrodollars to work, lent them to other developing countries, particularly those booming nations in Latin America. By 1982, Third World countries owed $500 billion in external debt, much of that to U.S. commercial banks. And with a worldwide recession, many developing countries could not service their obligations.

As of June 1982, when the crisis hit full force, 25 percent of U.S. commercial banks' international activity was in developing countries that sought debt rescheduling. Because of highly leveraged lending, the nine U.S. money center banks had lent the equivalent of almost two times their total capital worth to those countries, according to the *AMEX Bank Review*.[1]

Economic adjustment programs designed to help developing countries pay their debts have created new problems. American political leaders worry that Third World austerity programs, which typically eliminate subsidies for food and other commodities, will politically destabilize Latin American countries trying to restore democratic institutions. Further, needing to husband foreign exchange to service debts, Third World borrowers have cut back

---

1. *The AMEX Bank Review* 13 (October 1, 1985): p. 9. The World Bank estimates long-term developing country debt in 1982 as $546.89 billion and in 1985 as $708 billion. *World Debt Tables: External Debt of Developing Countries 1985-1986* (Washington, D.C.: World Bank, 1986), p. xii.

on imports, which hurts American farmers and manufacturers.

Ironically, the United States for much of its history was in the position that many developing countries are in today. Americans were net importers of capital until the early part of this century. In the 19th century the states of Pennsylvania, Maryland, Louisiana, and Mississippi defaulted on foreign loans. America, wrote an Englishman who had invested in Pennsylvania bonds, was "a nation with whom no contract can be made, because none will be kept."[2]

When U.S. banks began to open overseas branches just before World War I, they gravitated toward developing countries, particularly in Latin America, where Europeans had not yet penetrated and investments were growing. Today, rankings of banks by their international lending put U.S. institutions in four of the top five spots. Altogether some 200 U.S. banks make foreign loans, and numerous smaller banks play a critical role in supporting trade.

Big bank deals overseas continue despite—and sometimes because of—Third World debt problems. Bankers Trust Co. agreed at the end of 1985 to exchange Chilean foreign debt for equity in two of the country's financial firms. Scared by financial troubles at home, Latin American investors have deposited their money in U.S. banks. According to the *Journal of Commerce*, this "capital flight" raised foreign deposits in Miami to near record levels in 1985. While many American banks are looking to establish lending operations overseas, foreign banks are making inroads in the United States. Many American businesses have begun to shop abroad for financing. "Companies are paying less attention to geography and more to the attractiveness of deals in arranging financing," says Patrick J. Davey of the Conference Board.

Anyone wanting to trace bank connections overseas can start by examining the "Consolidated Domestic and Foreign Reports of Condition" that banks file quarterly with the Federal Deposit Insurance Corporation. These are available through the FDIC's Data Base Section. The Federal Financial Institutions Examina-

---

2. Anthony Sampson, *The Money Lenders: Bankers in a Dangerous World* (London: Coronet Books, 1981), pp. 54-55.

tion Council can give advice on how to use and acquire bank reports.

Some of the most interesting examples of the complexity of bank interdependence, however, can be found right on Main Street with banks that have never made foreign loans. "Even if a bank doesn't have foreign loans of its own," says Hugh Conway, an FDIC examiner, "that doesn't mean its welfare isn't dependent on world trade." The following story on a bank in Lincoln, Neb., explains why.

# Lincoln Bank Sows Third World Trade

LINCOLN, Neb.—Like international bankers generally, Brad Korell is worried about the more than $550 billion in commercial bank debts that Third World countries have piled up. Unlike big-city bankers, however, Korell, vice president of the National Bank of Commerce (NBC) here, is not afraid that Brazil, Argentina, Nigeria, and other debt-strapped countries will default.

Korell worries that the big money center banks won't lend them *more* money.

NBC does not make foreign loans like the ones that distress Chase Manhattan and Citicorp. But local clients, for whom it performs a variety of international services, have become heavily dependent on robust trade with developing countries. And today that trade is suffering because Third World nations cannot get sufficient financial resources to resume the high growth rates of the 1970s.

"I'm not personally worried about the money center banks," says Korell of the possibility of huge Third World defaults. "The government would bail the banks out.''

The bigger problem is that worried commercial banks have pulled back sharply on new lending, making the Third World's $100 billion annual obligations on long-term debt service all the more difficult an economic burden. ''If we extract everything out of developing countries in the short run,'' Korell says, ''we will destroy those markets for export products.''

His fears echo recent Treasury Department concerns about lack of growth in developing countries and the need to step up capital flows abroad. They also illustrate the special international orientation of local banks across the United States.

With about $425 million in assets, family-owned NBC is a smaller regional bank. Ranked by deposits, it is the fifth largest in the state and about 550 out of 14,000 in the country. The bank has no foreign offices, and barely a hint of international activity shows up on the lengthy financial reports it submits regularly to the federal government.

But a typical day for the three-member international department headed by Paul Warfield, 26, is busy from the time the guard brings up a briefcase full of currencies from Mexico, Great Britain, and other countries until the time the staff exits the building, designed by I.M. Pei's international architectural firm.

Lincolnites about to travel abroad buy the foreign currency. Foreign students at the University of Nebraska here purchase bank drafts in Indian rupees and Nigerian naira to send home. Customers wanting gold and silver coins from China, Mexico, and South Africa can order them at NBC.

The fastest growing part of the business lies in letters of credit, a kind of insurance policy banks provide for international transactions. A letter of credit, arranged by an importer's bank with a bank in the exporter's country, guarantees payment as soon as the merchandise arrives at its destination.

The largest share of this business—and one dependent on healthy trade with the developing world—is in helping firms like T-L Irrigation Co. in Hastings, which exports to Venezuela, Jordan, Brazil, and Saudi Arabia.

Letters of credit are especially important when doing business with developing countries where ''it's harder to know your customer or check him out," says Paul Warfield.

"You wouldn't be able to function on an international level without the bank," says an executive at Li-Cor Inc., a Lincoln firm that manufactures high-tech agricultural equipment sold widely in developing countries.

Although exports of irrigation equipment and grain bins have fallen off in the wake of economic troubles abroad, the 300 letters of credit passing over Warfield's desk this year are more than triple the number in 1982. About two-thirds involve Third World countries.

The international department, started in 1974, is now a profit center, says Korell, who is responsible for all NBC corporate banking.

Larger commercial banks asked NBC to participate in syndicated commercial loans to developing countries in the 1970s, when such lending was glamorous. NBC declined, Korell says, because it does not have the foreign expertise to risk deviating from its generally conservative strategy.

The closest it comes to foreign lending is to finance local export-related sales covered by the federally operated Export-Import Bank in Washington, D.C. Ex-Im can subsidize loan interest rates and provide risk insurance.

The Ex-Im transaction that Korell is most proud of was the sale to the Chinese of a hog confinement facility from Sand Livestock Systems in Columbus. The $300,000 deal was made through a Filipino entrepreneur, who planned to sell the pork in Hong Kong.

Defaults have recently resulted on NBC loans involving Bolivia and Mexico. Thanks to Ex-Im protection, the bank experienced only nominal losses, Korell says.

NBC's continuing interest in helping Nebraskans use the Ex-Im Bank reflects a trend by "more and more smaller banks," says Arthur Obester, a spokesman for the agency in Washington.

Large money center banks in Chicago and New York provide the same services as NBC on a grander, more sophisticated scale. But local businesses often prefer to conduct their international transactions through NBC.

NBC gives "personalized service," says Dan Kubit, con-

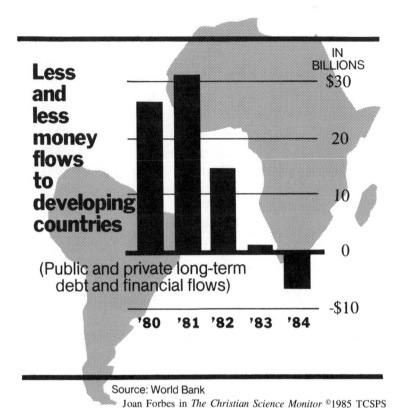

**Less and less money flows to developing countries**

(Public and private long-term debt and financial flows)

IN BILLIONS
$30
20
10
0
-$10

'80 '81 '82 '83 '84

Source: World Bank
Joan Forbes in *The Christian Science Monitor* ©1985 TCSPS

troller of Chief Industries, a manufacturer of grain bins and other products in Grand Island. Officers at larger banks frequently won't return Kubit's telephone calls the same day. But Paul Warfield is always available, even if he is on the road, and he can usually conclude a transaction on the telephone because he knows Kubit's voice.

This same personalized attention is a critical ingredient in getting small businesses beyond their initial fears about trading overseas. Warfield, whose family owns several smaller banks in the state, shows companies how to do paperwork and manage risks ''so they don't get burned on their first transaction and won't export again.''

In Lincoln, banks also provide an invaluable communications link with Third World countries, where telephones often don't work well and mails are slow. A local travel agency that arranges safaris in East Africa uses the bank's telex to transfer funds to

Nairobi, Kenya, make room reservations, and send personal messages.

Korell, who grew up on a farm in southwestern Nebraska, sees a bright future in international banking but is aware of the risks that have come with an increasingly interdependent world.

Massive defaults by just one or two of the big debtor Third World countries would threaten the industrialized world's major commercial banks. The health of those banks, whose network of services is responsible for the orderly flow of money, is an issue for the "entire Western banking system," he says.

Just a sag in Third World trade can hurt NBC, as has become painfully obvious. A decade ago NBC went years without a farm-related default. Today 60 percent of its defaults involve farmers, who have seen exports drop in part because indebted Third World countries have had to cut back on importing. The strong dollar and increased world competition have also hurt U.S. farm exports.

Sixteen of Nebraska's 455 banks closed this year and last, says Mary White of the Nebraska Bankers Association. "The closings relate directly to the depressed state of agricultural commodities."

*Cities serviced by National Bank of Commerce in Lincoln*

Joan Forbes in *The Christian Science Monitor*
©1985 TCSPS

White says state bank regulators expect additional closings in the coming months.

Last month the Treasury advanced a plan to restore the economic health of developing countries. It called for more lending by multilateral lending institutions such as the World Bank, better financial management by Third World countries, and $20 billion in additional loans by commercial banks ($7 billion by U.S. banks) over the next three years.

Last year Third World countries paid $7 billion more to commercial banks in long-term debt servicing than they received in comparable new loans. According to Nick Hope, an expert on world debt, that trend seems likely to accelerate this year.

Korell says he hasn't heard enough to know if the Treasury proposal will work.

But, he says, "the most interesting things banks do are to help other people do the things they do." And that, he believes, will be stymied for NBC if Third World countries don't grow.

**—John Maxwell Hamilton**
*The Christian Science Monitor*
November 12, 1985

# 8

# Third World Investment: Here and There

IN THE MID-1980s, The Associated Press reported that Indian immigrants, many named Patel, had bought up thousands of motels, particularly in the South and Southwest. In Texas alone, Patel-owned motels outnumbered Holiday Inns 429 to 133. According to one estimate, Indians or people of Indian descent owned 28 percent of the nation's motels and hotels.[1]

The immediate story behind the story is that Indians coming to the United States had discovered they could get into the motel business with a small investment. And when the word got around back home, especially in Gujarat state in West India where Patel is a common name, the investment stampede began.

The long-range story behind the story is that it is becoming hard to tell where borders begin and where they end when the subject is investment.

The 24-hour-a-day global stock market has emerged. Wall Street investors who like to work when the sun goes down can spend their nights buying stock options and precious metals in Singapore and Hong Kong. Citicorp and McGraw-Hill have recently made overseas trading easier. They now jointly offer a computerized global information service that also allows subscribers to trade and arrange financing day and night.

An increasing number of mutual funds specialize in foreign stocks, and in 1983 and 1984, Americans bought $5 billion more in foreign stocks than they sold, according to *Fortune*. "Today,

---

1. AP stories by Scott McCartney, October 18, 1984, and Elliott Minor, June 11, 1985.

over 325 companies' shares are actively trading in more than one country,'' Securities and Exchange Commission Chairman John Shad said in 1985. ''It seems inevitable that within a year or two, a multiple of that will be trading around the clock and the world, through a grid of networks that interconnect the major markets.''

Foreigners purchasing U.S. securities and depositing funds in U.S. banks made it easier for the Reagan administration to finance budget deficits and keep down inflation. Roger Brinner, an economist with Data Resources Inc., estimated in 1984 that these financial flows funded more than 25 percent of corporate capital spending in the United States, according to a *New York Times* report. Latin America provided about a fifth of these funds.

The search for tax havens offers a special kind of investment story. Many small Third World countries have small tax bases. As a result they have much to gain from imposing low taxes and relaxing financial reporting requirements, conditions that attract foreign investors who wish to shelter their resources. After looking at the Oxford International Bank & Trust Co., Ltd., in the Turks and Caicos Islands, British West Indies, Senate staff investigators concluded that ''offshore banking accounts are being used by people one might regard as 'average American citizens.' ''[2]

In the area of plant and equipment investment overseas, the United States is the world's largest investor and has been for years. Of more recent significance is the changed attitude toward investing in the Third World—and the beginnings of Third World investments in the United States.

One sign of change is the trend toward U.S. investment in Third World manufacturing facilities rather than just in exploitation of natural resources. ''You have to compete with world labor rates and compete against foreign manufacturers which have lower wages,'' James O'Connor, president of the American Optical Co., told *The News*, in Southbridge, Mass., ''You just have to be in more than one location in order to even things out.''

Venture capitalists have also begun to look overseas. In 1985, they ''raised nearly $80 million from U.S. corporations to invest overseas,'' reported *The Wall Street Journal*. ''The total for the

---

2. Senate Committee on Governmental Affairs, *Crime and Secrecy: The Use of Offshore Banks and Companies: Hearings before the Permanent Subcommittee on Investigations*, 1983.

prior four years was only $120 million.'' Although most of that investment went to the United Kingdom, investors are also interested in Southeast Asia.

Most developing countries do not have the surplus funds to make large investments overseas. But as their economies grow and as they look for new ways to participate in the U.S. economy and avoid protectionist barriers here, their investments are likely to pick up. Already some big deals have been struck. In 1985, U.S. Steel announced it would form a joint venture with South Korea to modernize its Pittsburg, Calif., steel plant. English, Japanese, and Brazilian investors joined to revive the Fontana Steel Mill in California that same year.

The stories below tell both sides of the direct investment story. The first, set in Beaverton, Ore., examines Third World investments by a company that would just as soon have stayed out of developing countries—but couldn't without losing its competitiveness. The second, set in Dallas, relates a new worry about Third World investors in this country: that they aren't investing enough.

The federal government has plenty of people who can help put stories like these together. The Commerce Department Office of International Investment keeps lists of foreign manufacturing investments here. Foreigners are required to report all land purchases. The Agriculture Department keeps the records. As for locating U.S. investors in the Third World, one place to start is the Overseas Private Investment Corp., which insures smaller companies (those not on the Fortune 1000 list) making investments in developing countries.

# Beaverton Firm Exploring Joint Ventures Abroad

BEAVERTON, Ore.—Tektronix likes to think of itself as a local company. It considers its 20,000 employees, nearly 70 percent of whom are within a 30-mile radius of this Portland suburb, part of a closely knit family.

But when it comes to investing in future growth, Tektronix is broadening that family to include men and women in places as globally diverse as Shanghai, Bombay, and Saõ Paulo.

The manufacturer of electronic instrumentation is currently investing time and money to work with firms in India, China, and Brazil, which are starting to make its low-cost oscilloscopes under license. A wholly owned sales and service office in Hong Kong will start up operations in June. Tektronix has provided capital for a Chinese-run service center in Beijing and opened its own sales office in that city last year with about half a dozen employees.

Tektronix is considering several other possibilities, including joint ventures, in developing countries. In China alone, says Duane Bowans, who manages Tektronix's operations there, "we are probably juggling 3 or 4 other technical projects. . . . We are going to do some conservative equity investment in China."

Investments like these give Tektronix and other companies access to foreign markets and low-cost labor. They give Third World countries access to capital and to training and technology.

"They are young, they are hungry, and they are literate," says Senior Vice President John L. Landis about especially attractive markets in newly industrializing countries like many along the Pacific Rim. "You better participate in some of that.

"There should be a payoff for everybody."

Tektronix has been keenly interested in foreign sales since

shortly after two Oregonians founded the company in 1946, says general counsel R. Allan Leedy Jr. About 40 percent of its nearly $1.5 billion in annual sales are currently overseas.

Tektronix has owned manufacturing facilities in Europe for nearly three decades, and it invested with Sony in an assembly operation in Japan 20 years ago. A joint venture in Mexico and a wholly owned subsidiary in Brazil handle sales and distribution.

But Tektronix—the largest employer in Oregon—has been conservative about making foreign investments, Leedy says.

It has not yet set up plants in developing countries to make products at a lower cost, something many electronics companies have done.

The overall financial outlays in its license arrangements are relatively small. The biggest cost, Landis says, is in travel and training and other activities required in assisting the offshore company to start production.

The costs for starting a sales and service office like the one starting up in Hong Kong can range from $300,000 to $10 million, says Landis, who attributes the biggest cost to operating capital required after the doors open.

Landis expects the subsidiary to be in the black in two years and self-financing in four.

That Tektronix has felt the need to make even these modest investments, however, is a sign of the times. The increasing integration of the world economy to include developing countries requires American business to invest resources overseas, often in ways that they never before considered.

Early in this century developing countries, like those in Latin America, were prime spots for U.S. investors interested in capitalizing on minerals and other natural resources they could export to industrialized countries. After World War II, those developing countries wanted control over their resources. They expropriated foreign holdings and restricted foreign investments.

Those trends discouraged American business from making new Third World investments. U.S. direct investments in the Third World dropped from one-half of the overseas total in 1950 to about 25 percent in 1984.

Now investors have begun to change attitudes about at least

some developing countries. And although they are not about to relinquish control over their resources, some developing countries are keen to see these new investments, as Tektronix's recent activities show.

—India is trying to give added energy to its economy. Leaders promise economic reforms that include greater freedom to private enterprises and more open trade. Among other things, they have reduced import and export duties and simplified procedures for investors.

India's large population offers a potentially important market, Leedy says. Tektronix has begun to look at investment opportunities beyond its recent license arrangement.

—Brazil still has tough regulations over foreign investment that worry companies like Tektronix that do not want to lose control of their technology. But the country also offers a promising long-term market.

Tektronix decided on a license arrangement because it involved the lowest investment while giving the company "a way of getting our toe in the water in Brazil," Leedy says.

—Likewise, the new open door to China has rekindled visions of large profits for many American companies.

The Chinese interest in using television as a vehicle for widespread public education has led to an informal sharing of Tektronix's technology for calibrating colors on television cameras. Stephen D. Kerman, a Tektronix marketing director who works on the project, believes this early collaboration will lead to a formal licensing agreement with the Chongqing Radio Test Instrument Factory to produce the equipment.

Although Tektronix executives admit they are thinking about opening a manufacturing facility in the Third World, low labor costs have not been as important to them as they are to other companies.

Tektronix's niche is largely in the high-quality, low-volume market, not in mass production, Leedy says. "We have been cut off at the pass selling high volume stuff."

In addition, Tektronix has been able to reduce labor requirements through automation. "Every time we bring out a new generation of oscilloscopes, we cut the labor by a factor of 2 to 4, maybe more,'' Landis says.

From a strictly economic point of view, Landis says, ''the best way I can get products to India is to export.''

Selling overseas, however, often means producing overseas. Tektronix set up its subsidiaries in Europe in order to avoid tariff barriers. Today, Bowans points out, developing countries are ''saying we'll buy some of your products, but as a ticket to that, we want some of your technology.''

For Tektronix that means helping the Chinese use the technology in their own country. Its first license agreement in China is with the 21st Radio Factory of Shanghai.

In the early stages the Chinese carry out simple assembly procedures on Tektronix's basic oscilloscope. Later they will perform more sophisticated assembly operations and even learn to produce some of the components in their own country, Tektronix officials say.

Tektronix opened a service center in Beijing in 1983, run under contract by the Chinese Academy of Science. The company provided about $200,000 in capital to equip and train 11 Chinese.

''I think this is the real foreign aid,'' Landis says. ''The government doesn't have the technology to transfer.''

For its part, Tektronix profits from the sale of its license plus from the subsequent sale of parts. It also gains a foothold in the Chinese market, which is highly sought after by Japanese competitors.

In the short term, this can mean more employment for American workers who produce components to be assembled. In the case of its China operation, Tektronix has set up a special support unit with five employees in Beaverton.

The long term is more complex, Tektronix executives say.

''You are, by definition, developing somebody who will someday be a competitor,'' Landis says.

This puts enormous pressure on Tektronix to continually produce more sophisticated technology that will be in demand in China.

But as Landis sees it, "As the country develops, it gives us other business opportunities."

**—John Maxwell Hamilton**
*The Christian Science Monitor*
May 12, 1986

# Dallas Wants More Foreign Investments

DALLAS—During the last 1970s, Americans worried that oil-rich OPEC countries would buy the United States and control production of food, energy, and products.

It hasn't happened. Although investment from OPEC countries has increased almost 30-fold since 1975, the total amount is still small. OPEC countries pose no threat to the Dallas-Fort Worth economy.

Instead of rejoicing, some Dallas executives wish investment by OPEC members and other less-developed countries was on the rise, creating jobs and propping up the sagging real estate market.

"I have never had so many calls as I have had in the last two weeks from sellers who are hunting foreign buyers," said Max Hatfield, a Henry S. Miller Co. broker.

OPEC's economic stake in the United States is minimal. Its direct investment, for example, in manufacturing and real estate increased to 3 percent in 1981 from less than 1 percent of total foreign investment in 1975, according to Department of Commerce data. Since then, OPEC's share hasn't changed.

Latin American countries have accounted for about 10 percent of direct foreign investment since 1980. They accounted for less than 1 percent in 1975.

"As a whole, LDC investment in this country is minimal. And if you take out the oil investment of LDCs, it wouldn't even show up," said Jeff Ardan, director of the International Business Program at the University of South Carolina and author of a book on foreign investment in the United States.

Altogether, foreigners own only a tiny part of the U.S. economy—1.3 percent of its $11.9 trillion in assets, according to Federal Reserve Bank data.

Texas has more foreign investment in property, plant, and equipment than any other state and ranks third in foreign investment in agricultural land, according to the Department of Commerce.

Some purchases have been large and dramatic. Two weeks ago, for example, Arab investors bought the tallest building in Texas, the 75-story Texas Commerce Bank building in Houston. And Venezuela's state-owned oil company is putting the final touches on an agreement to buy half of Dallas-based Southland Corp.'s Citgo refinery.

Despite these flashy buys, foreigners play only a bit part in the local economy. Statewide, foreign investment in Texas real estate was $5.3 billion in 1982, according to the Commerce Department. That's about the same amount of investment that Dallas real estate developer Trammell Crow currently has nationwide.

Moreover, European and Canadian investors—not OPEC or other developing countries—have traditionally been the biggest buyers of U.S. real estate, said Ken Shulman, executive vice president of Henry S. Miller Co.

"Foreigners—no matter where they are from—always own a very, very small portion of the market," Shulman said. "They tend to buy what I call critical pieces of real estate. But all it takes is two or three of these big real estate deals to change hands, and everyone thinks there is a conspiracy."

Ghaith Pharaon, a Saudi Arabian investor, provided grist for the rumor mill in 1978 when he helped fund the swank Plaza of the Americas Hotel, valued at $100 million. Pharaon's invest-

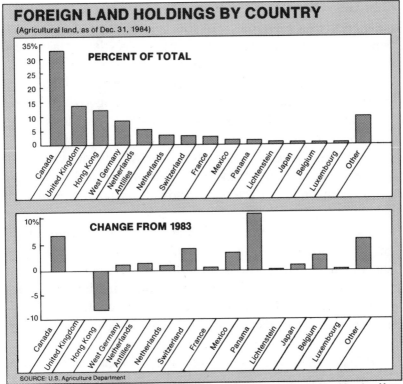

**FOREIGN LAND HOLDINGS BY COUNTRY**
(Agricultural land, as of Dec. 31, 1984)

PERCENT OF TOTAL

CHANGE FROM 1983

SOURCE: U.S. Agriculture Department

*The Dallas Morning News*

ments, which ranged from banks to contracting companies, sparked speculation that he would continue to buy companies.

Pharaon didn't gobble up other high-profile investments, and the furor quieted. "There are always those crazy concerns about the threat of the foreigners. That 'threat' then never comes to fruition," Shulman said.

In fact, foreigners have been selling. "Most of my investors sold their properties because the dollar was so strong—they had a good return just on the currency exchange."

Foreign real estate investment in the area is now at its lowest point in almost 10 years, said investment advisers who work with offshore buyers.

Dallas County has few acres of agricultural land, but investors from developing countries in Tarrant County own more than 3,000 acres valued at $27.7 million, according to records filed with the Department of Agriculture.

Investors from countries such as Panama and the Netherlands Antilles accounted for much of the land purchased in Tarrant County. Low taxes and strong banking-secrecy laws make these countries havens for investors from other countries.

Developing countries have opened sales, service, and packaging operations in Dallas and Fort Worth, according to a 1985 Price Waterhouse survey. There are 24 Third World countries, ranging from China to Argentina, represented in the survey.

Among the larger investments is the government of Kuwait's purchase of Santa Fe International, a California-based energy and mineral company. Its Dallas subsidiary, Santa Fe Minerals, employs 400 people.

A hard-to-trace but "significant" source of foreign investment is the capital that flows into banks and stocks, said Richard Fisher, senior manager at Brown Brothers Harriman.

"We know that there is $30 to $35 billion in Mexican money outside of Mexico. A significant portion is in contiguous states, mainly in California and Texas. It is reasonable to assume a portion of that significant portion is in Dallas," he said.

Investors often send their money to the United States to escape political and economic risk at home.

John Cuddington, an economist with the World Bank, said most of the capital flight comes from troubled countries such as Argentina, Mexico, Venezuela, Uruguay, and recently, from the Philippines. "There are traces of (Philippine money) already in our own city," Fisher said.

The new Philippine government charged earlier this month that deposed President Ferdinand Marcos owns real estate reportedly valued at $13 million in Tarrant County.

Many of the developing countries try to keep the capital at home through strict controls, Cuddington said. Capital flight saps money for investment for the developing country and erodes the tax base.

Wealthy citizens can find ways around the laws, he said. "They feel that it is in their private interest to take money out— even though the country itself is in need of capital."

Strapped by debt and low growth rates, many developing countries need money to finance their own development, South

Carolina's Ardan said.

"Developing countries just don't have a whole lot of money to invest," Ardan said. Even the OPEC countries are making fewer new investments, now that oil prices and revenues have plunged.

Rebounding oil prices will spur foreign investment, said Ms. Michael Goodwin, a Commerce Department economist.

"I wouldn't count out OPEC countries," Fisher said. "When the real estate market gets weak, we will see a renewed interest from Kuwait and other Arab countries."

The newly industrialized countries (NICs) in East Asia are potential investors. The economies of Taiwan, Hong Kong, South Korea, and Singapore have grown rapidly in recent years, even while other developing nations—particularly in Africa—have slipped backward.

"Now we find a surge in Asian investment," said Christine Klepacz of the Commerce Department. "It has to do with 20 years of growth, so they have money to invest."

NICs can use their investment to develop markets in the United States, gain access to technology, and avoid trade barriers, Klepacz said. The relatively stable U.S. economy attracts Hong Kong investors who worry about what will happen when the British colony reverts to the communist People's Republic of China.

LDCs only open U.S. operations when it is to their economic advantage, Ardan said. Low labor costs often make it more profitable for countries such as Taiwan and South Korea to keep manufacturing operations at home, he said.

Initial investments can be used as a base for expansion. Korean-owned Hyundai Furniture Industries in Dallas is considering an investment in the eastern part of the United States, plant manager Scott F. Minter said.

The Kuwait government has increased by more than a third its original investment in Santa Fe International, said Boyd Hight, executive vice president of the company. The parent company has doubled the number of employees, said Lyle Livingstone, president of Santa Fe International's Dallas-based subsidiary.

In contrast to the pervasive fears during the late 1970s, many Dallas business leaders hope foreign investment will pick up.

# FOREIGN INVESTMENT

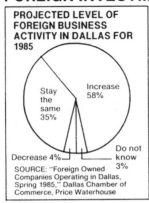

**PROJECTED LEVEL OF FOREIGN BUSINESS ACTIVITY IN DALLAS FOR 1985**

Increase 58%

Stay the same 35%

Decrease 4%

Do not know 3%

SOURCE: "Foreign Owned Companies Operating in Dallas, Spring 1985," Dallas Chamber of Commerce, Price Waterhouse

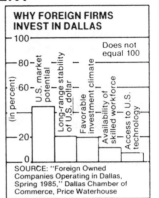

**WHY FOREIGN FIRMS INVEST IN DALLAS**

Does not equal 100

(in percent)

- U.S. market potential
- Long-range stability of U.S. dollar
- Favorable investment climate
- Availability of skilled workforce
- Access to U.S. technology

SOURCE: "Foreign Owned Companies Operating in Dallas, Spring 1985," Dallas Chamber of Commerce, Price Waterhouse

## FOREIGN INVESTMENT IN U.S. INDUSTRY

(Investments made in 1984 by sector)

| Sector | Value in millions | Percent of total | Change from '83 |
|---|---|---|---|
| Petroleum | $3,080 | 23.7% | +681.7% |
| Manufacturing | $2,471 | 19.0 | -20.6 |
| Real estate | $1,510 | 11.6 | -43.2 |
| Retail trade | $1,021 | 7.8 | +974.7 |
| Mining | $806 | 6.2 | +2,078.4 |
| Banking | $803 | 6.2 | +364.2 |
| Wholesale trade | $761 | 5.8 | +284.3 |
| Finance | $741 | 5.7 | +62.1 |
| Insurance | $149 | 1.1 | +23.1 |
| TOTAL | $13,018 | 100.0 | +60.9 |

SOURCE: U.S. Department of Commerce

## FOREIGN HOLDINGS OF AGRICULTURAL LAND

(Top states, as of December 31, 1984. Acres in thousands, dollar values in billions)

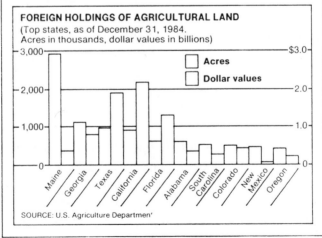

■ Acres

□ Dollar values

Maine, Georgia, Texas, California, Florida, Alabama, South Carolina, Colorado, New Mexico, Oregon

SOURCE: U.S. Agriculture Departmen'

*The Dallas Morning News*

Foreign capital could refinance part of the 90 million square feet of vacant commercial space in the city.

But real estate broker Michael Young, who worked with many of the Canadian firms that made investments in Dallas a few years ago, said factors that have soured domestic investors' attitudes toward Sun Belt property also scare off foreign buyers. "A typical foreign investor looking for a safe place for his capital has not felt like this has been a particularly safe market."

Dallas needs the investment to increase employment, pump up the economy, and increase the city's international ties, said Chris D. Simpson, partner at Price Waterhouse.

R. Richard Rubottom, director of the Dallas Office of International Affairs and former ambassador to Argentina, agreed: "This is a wonderful time to reach out and attract that foreign investment."

—**Todd Vogel and John Maxwell Hamilton**
**with a contribution by Steve Brown**
*The Dallas Morning News*
March 16, 1986

# 9

# Foreign Aid: How It's Helping Americans

*"You know, sometimes the P.L. 480 American food aid program gets criticized for having created dependencies overseas and creating reliance on the program. . . . It is often not stated that those of us in many of the ports have also grown, for better or worse, reliant on the P.L. 480 program."*—Davis Helberg[1]

ALTHOUGH FOREIGN AID is often called "a cause without a constituency," the money that Congress appropriates each year to help developing countries benefits a wide variety of American constituencies: universities, whose faculties study development problems; manufacturers, who supply the brick and mortar used in development projects; architectural and engineering firms, who help design and oversee the construction of roads and schools; farmers, who grow food to send to hungry people; and, as Helberg noted, numerous intermediates, including those who load and transport food aid.

Even private aid organizations working overseas rely on government-run foreign aid programs. The Salvation Army, Catholic Relief Services, the Helen Keller Institute, and the AFL-CIO's American Institute for Free Labor Development, among other groups, use foreign aid dollars to carry on their work. According to the American Council for Voluntary International Action, the federal government's Food for Peace program supported nearly one-half the African famine assistance provided

---

1. Statement of Davis Helberg, executive director, Seaway Port Authority of Duluth, before House Merchant Marine Subcommittee, October 31, 1985.

through voluntary organizations by the end of 1985. The U.S. Agency for International Development provided another 10 percent in grants and contracts.

Private voluntary organizations, with offices around the country, can explain their work overseas. AID and the World Bank publish annual listings of their purchases of goods and services in the United States. The reports, broken down by state, identify the companies and organizations from which purchases were made. AID and the U.S. Department of Agriculture jointly oversee the Food for Peace program. Their statistics were used to put together the following story on a community in Minnesota that has benefited from food aid.

# Food Aid Puts Duluth To Work

DULUTH, Minn.—The people who work along the docks of Lake Superior know that there is more to U.S. food aid than feeding hungry people abroad.

"We feed the world, but we are also feeding ourselves," says the Rev. Norbert Mokros, a former commissioner of the Seaway Port Authority of Duluth and pastor of a center for seafarers.

Located at the western tip of the Great Lakes, Duluth and its neighbor, Superior, Wis., are a shipping point for food given away or purchased with low-interest loans under the U.S. foreign aid program.

This year Food for Peace, as it is called, accounts for about 90 percent of the export shipping done by the publicly owned Seaway Port Authority and the privately owned Meehan Seaway Service in Superior. These are the only two local operations that can handle processed bagged food sent to needy Third World countries.

Food for Peace is only one-twentieth of the port's total export business, which is predominantly bulk cargo sold by General Mills and other large dealers. But food aid takes on disproportionate importance to longshoremen, who make their livings all along the waterfront.

Longshoremen can quickly pour unprocessed grain onto ships. They must load bagged food by hand.

During the last seven years, Food for Peace shipments accounted for about one-half of the working hours put in by longshoremen, according to Port Authority calculations.

Every ton of food aid pumps $85 into the local economy, almost three times as much as a ton of bulk grain, Port Authority Director Davis Helberg says.

Not surprisingly, officials like Helberg are deeply troubled by slippage of Duluth's share of this cargo as a result of competing interests wanting to profit from the food aid business. Food for Peace, observes Mokros, is a "hot political item."

From the beginning, self-interest has been a major element in Public Law 480, the legislation that created the Food for Peace program in 1954. By helping poor countries meet short-term food needs, Congress saw a way of disposing of surplus agricultural products and acquiring long-term customers.

Administered by the USDA and AID, P.L. 480 has provided an effective outlet for surpluses, at its high point in the early 1960s accounting for 25 percent of the dollar value of U.S. farm exports. Today Food for Peace amounts to less than 5 percent of total agricultural exports, but has been responsible for over 60 percent of the exports of wheat flour and non-fat dry milk, two of the 100 commodities supported by the program.

Although recipient countries in the Third World can lean on food assistance to avoid steps to increase their own domestic food production, "P.L. 480's batting average is very high" as a developmental tool, says Dr. John W. Mellor, director of the International Food Policy Research Institute in Washington. "Countries that are doing well in domestic agriculture production now were major recipients of food aid."

Third World economic growth has made developing countries good markets for U.S. farm exports. The 16 developing countries with the highest growth rates in their basic food staples in

*Surprising as it may seem, Duluth in America's heartland is a major port for foreign aid.*

Joan Forbes in *The Christian Science Monitor*
©1985 TCSPS

the 1960s and 1970s doubled their imports in those same products, Mellor says.

In response to the African famine, Congress increased P.L. 480 last year by more than 30 percent to $2.2 billion. About half was sent as outright donations.

Loans to help developing countries purchase U.S. grain carry interest rates of 3 percent to 7 percent and repayment periods of up to 40 years for the poorest nations.

Duluth and Superior began shipping Food for Peace commodities when the St. Lawrence Seaway opened Great Lakes ports to world commerce in 1959. The most important commodities for the ports are bulgur wheat, which is processed about 550 miles away in Crete, Neb., and non-fat dry milk produced in the upper Midwest, says Alan T. Johnson, director of international marketing for the Duluth Port Authority.

Even with increases in P.L. 480, Food for Peace shipments out of Duluth-Superior have declined for three straight years. Port officials attribute this to a variety of factors, including cargo preference rules.

Under federal regulations written by Congress, at least 50 percent of all shipments of government-generated exports, including Food for Peace, have had to travel on U.S. flag ships. Legislation in the farm bill, which is to be signed by President Reagan today, aims to increase U.S. shippers' share of P.L. 480 to 75 percent over the next three years.

With the decline of the shipping industry, only one U.S.

ocean-going line still travels regularly into the Great Lakes, reducing Duluth's prospects of handling food aid.

Duluthians feel that they have a right to handle a larger share of Food for Peace exports. "If you are paying taxes you are entitled to P.L. 480 cargoes," says Peter Harris, manager of Meehan Seaway Service.

Just as shippers get a preference to help them stay in business, "there should be an exclusion for the Great Lakes," says Bob Picard, president of the Superior International Longshoreman Association. "As a result of them protecting their jobs, we're losing ours."

Another problem is competition. "P.L. 480 used to be gravy for ports like Houston and New Orleans," Helberg says. Now, with agricultural exports declining as a result of Third World economic troubles, "they have been going after it with both feet."

To make itself more competitive, Meehan Seaway Service added grain storage facilities this year and, with government financial help, will shortly start dredging a deeper slip, making it possible for ships to take on more cargo.

With help from the city, the Duluth Port Authority has purchased equipment for bagging grain. Although Helberg does not think the equipment will be used exclusively for food aid, its first job was to bag food purchased with $350,000 in private Minnesota donations. The food left Duluth this month for East Africa.

Also on the vessel were 800 bags of wood briquettes made by a Minnesota company out of sawdust and wood chips. World Vision, an international relief organization, will test the wood as fuel in Sudan. The Port Authority, a marketing firm, and the shipping line are underwriting the cost of the shipment.

Use of such fuels could be an answer to deforestation in developing countries and an outlet for surplus timber in Minnesota and Wisconsin, Helberg says. With a successful test, he hopes that AID and other development institutions will purchase the briquettes for shipment to the Third World.

The financing arrangements, he believes, could be the same as for P.L. 480.

—**John Maxwell Hamilton**
*The Christian Science Monitor*
December 23, 1985

# 10

# Homegrown Foreign Aid

ALTHOUGH AMERICANS benefit from government foreign aid programs, public support for aid is low. Even on the docks of Duluth, longshoremen and shipping agents question if food aid really helps other countries.

Yet, aid's low public esteem is misleading. Although polls on public attitudes toward aid present a welter of often incoherent data, they seem to indicate support for some kinds of assistance. In 1981, 74 percent of respondents to a Roper poll said something should be done to cut foreign economic aid. A 1979 Gallup poll for the Presidential Commission on World Hunger, however, found that 81 percent of respondents would maintain or increase that portion of their tax dollars going to alleviate world hunger.

Americans have a strong suspicion of any long-term, government-run aid program with an uncertain outcome. They have an equally strong impulse to help other, less-fortunate people, especially when the goals seem straightforward and the avenues of help seem to run through non-government channels. Evidence of that is visible in the American response to the recent African famine. A church in Belfry, Ky., contributed the bulk of a member's $125,000 donation to famine relief rather than pay off its mortgage; 200 inmates at the La Tune Federal Corrections Institution in Anthony, Texas, contributed $1,629 of their prison wages. A private organization in Vermont started its own version of the Peace Corps, giving citizens of the state a chance to work up to six months in Africa.

As the following story illustrates, when the people of Hattiesburg, Miss., did their part, it fit into a general community attitude about helping less-fortunate peoples. The story also offers a glimpse of the local stake in economic development abroad.

# Local Citizens Giving Generously To Poor Overseas

HATTIESBURG, Miss.—Last Christmas, Baptist missionaries Cora Joyce and Ralph Davis came home to Hattiesburg to tell about the severe drought in Ghana, where harvests for some farmers were down to 100 pounds of rice.

The Davises had used all their own savings to feed people around their mission and hoped they could raise $1,000 during their home leave to carry on the feeding program.

They underestimated South Mississippi generosity toward poor countries of the Third World.

After hearing Mrs. Davis talk, Temple Baptist made its largest annual foreign mission contribution ever, almost $18,000, and in March presented the Davises a separate check for $8,800.

Calvary Baptist, Petal-Harvey Baptist, First Baptist of Laurel, and members of the First Baptist and Main Street Baptist churches in Hattiesburg made additional contributions.

And when the Davises urged truck driver Glen Corley of Lumberton to come to Ghana to haul food and medicine, another round of contributions began.

Corley needed funds to fly to West Africa and to cover expenses for his family during the three months he would be gone. More than $8,000 came from Petal-Harvey Baptist, Indian Springs Baptist, Temple Baptist, 38th Avenue Baptist, Bellevue Baptist, and Olive Baptist—his church—as well as from a variety of individuals and organizations including Miller Transport, where Corley worked, Local 891 of the Teamsters union, and Teamsters President C. A. Davis.

In Ghana, Corley hauled his cargo 600 miles from the coast to the northern town of Nalerigu, a trip over roads so bad that it often took a week to complete the journey. When soldiers stopped him along the road, he speedily got past by giving them ballpoint pens donated by a bank in Purvis.

This response to the African famine illustrates that, while local support for U.S. foreign aid programs is often low, Hattiesburg and the surrounding communities believe in homegrown giving. Churches provide a large share of that help, but the private sector does its share too.

"Hattiesburg is conservative when it comes to government, but liberal when it comes to generosity," says John McGregor, a businessman who spends part of each summer doing missionary work in Mexico.

The South has long contributed missionaries for service as educators and doctors in Asia, Africa, and Latin America. Today the Southern Baptist Convention has more than 3,000 missionaries abroad, including many from South Mississippi, says Dr. Peter McLeod, pastor of First Baptist Church in Hattiesburg.

The Davises, Baptists who grew up in Macedonia, near Petal, have served in West Africa since 1950. Cora Joyce Davis is a registered nurse and works with Ghanaian women. Her husband is a teacher.

In addition to supporting parent organizations with annual financial contributions, local churches carry on their own missions. The Centerville Baptist Church organized a medical mission to Honduras earlier this year. The First Baptist Church of Hattiesburg sponsors an annual medical mission to Rio Dosa, Mexico, says Scotland-born McLeod, in addition to contributing about 10 percent of its $800,000 annual budget to foreign missionary activity.

Mississippi's two Catholic dioceses have supported a mission in Saltillo, Mexico, since 1969. Each month the Rev. Peter Quinn, a priest from the Biloxi diocese who runs the mission, distributes 30 tons of red beans, paid for by Mississippi Catholics, to 6,000 Mexican families. Catholics from Hattiesburg make special trips to help the parishioners of Saltillo each year.

Local business also plays a role—a role that is often both charitable and profitable.

On its own initiative, Cathodic Engineering, a Hattiesburg company that specializes in corrosion prevention processes, plans to train two Chinese from Beijing University. The idea came out of a trip to China by the chairman of Cathodic Engineering, Joe Tatum Sr. The Chinese will pay their own travel expenses. Cathodic Engineering will pay their salaries.

It's good business to help the Chinese, says Joe Tatum Jr., president of Cathodic Engineering. China has recently undertaken an ambitious economic development program, including modernization of its petroleum sector. Oil drilling typically requires extensive use of anti-corrosion technology to protect pipes.

"Like my daddy used to tell me," says the younger Tatum, "I never made a plug nickel off my enemies, but I've made a fortune off my friends."

Also seeing profit in good work, the Southern Center for Research and Innovation, a non-profit center seeking to enlarge business opportunities for the community, is developing a satellite-based, emergency communications system for the Pan American Health Organization. The portable terminals, worth $12,000, will allow PAHO headquarters to communicate with Caribbean regions during hurricanes and floods.

Dr. William Brundage, executive director of the research center, hopes that his organization will be able to make other sales abroad. A potential sale of medical technology used at the Forrest General Hospital to Saudi Arabia could amount to $20 million, says Brundage. Brundage also says that computer software technology currently under development, which includes programs to help tally votes in local elections, could find a market in the developing world.

Although such projects mean money for Hattiesburg, compassion seems to be a vital force behind local efforts to help developing nations. Businessmen belonging to the Hattiesburg Rotary Club, for example, make regular donations for overseas charity through the Rotary Foundation. One member, Dr. Milam Cotton, has contributed $4,000.

John McGregor, a native of Hattiesburg and president of McGregor Enterprises, perhaps best sums up local attitudes toward helping the Third World. McGregor, a member of St. Thomas Parish in Hattiesburg, drives his van 22,000 miles to Saltillo every summer to help the Catholic mission build houses or do other social projects.

"It's the most rewarding thing I do each year," he says, "by far, by far."

**—John Maxwell Hamilton**
*Hattiesburg American*
November 15, 1984.

# 11

## *"Hello, This Is Montego Bay"*

# The Information Revolution

"TECHNOLOGY CHANGES so quickly," a Commerce Department official says, "it's hard to know what will happen next." One thing is certain, though. The information revolution is shortening the distance between the Third World and Main Street America.

In another age, international businesses with overseas operations located themselves in commercial centers such as New York City or London. Today, CFL Ltd., a data entry firm with facilities in Montego Bay, Jamaica, is based in Camanche, Iowa. A.C. Nielsen has its coupon clearinghouse in Clinton, Iowa, although most of the actual coupon sorting and counting is done in Mexico and Haiti.

Just as the industrial revolution gave new meaning to the production of bolts of cloth and steel bars, the information revolution has transformed the services sector of the economy. American corporations commission Indians to write their computer programs. At the beginning of 1986 a midwestern businessman contemplated setting up the ultimate in cosmopolitan telephone-answering services. If a subscriber isn't home, an operator in Montego Bay will answer the telephone for him and take a message.

While it remains to be seen whether better global understanding will result from better communications, there is no doubt that manufacturers expect to profit. In February 1986, Chinese began to watch "One World," a series of 15-minute documentaries on international subjects produced in the United States. General Foods

Corp. was one of the sponsors. It hoped its commercials would convince the Chinese to drink Maxwell House Coffee.

The services sector of the American economy, which depends heavily on improved information flows, more than doubled between 1970 and 1985. Although the U.S. trade surplus in services has dwindled, Americans are still the world's foremost exporters of services, with major activities in advertising, banking, insurance, and investment. The Conference Board predicts that "virtually all U.S. job growth between now and the end of this century will be in services."

Future global developments likely to make a difference to the American service industry and to individual Americans depend both on agreements covering trade in services, an issue that came up at the GATT (General Agreement on Tariff and Trade) conference in 1986, and on adjustments in American regulations concerning information. How, for instance, should U.S. customs officials levy duties on imported information that has been processed in Third World countries? How should individuals' privacy be protected in transnational data flows? And what about protection of intellectual property: should U.S. copyrights be extended to books by U.S. authors printed and produced outside the United States?

The story below looks at some of these issues from the vantage point of Saztec, a data processing company in California. As the story notes, Saztec has computerized health records for 80 hospitals. A journalist in any one of those communities could put together a similar article.

# High-Tech Firm Has Data Center in Third World

ROLLING HILLS ESTATES, Calif.—Saztec Corp. is young and still small by the standards of giant multinationals. But its operational network is as complicated as the circuitry of a computer, one of the high-tech tools that is increasingly allowing it—and service industries like it—to use Third World workers.

Saztec processes information. Its headquarters is in a small pair of suites here, about 25 miles south of downtown Los Angeles. A partner in Hollywood takes microfilms of the information to be processed; a facility in Dayton, Ohio, handles the final steps needed to organize the information.

But when it comes to the enormous job in between—typing the raw data onto computer tapes—Saztec turns to workers in the Philippines, Singapore, and Jamaica.

Saztec's far-flung work force has "keyed" a wide range of information: circuit records needed in servicing 21 million telephone lines operated by Pacific Telephone; the texts of French novels and patent records for the European Economic Community; patient records for 80 hospitals from Greensboro, N.C., to Pomona, Calif.; and the compensation and perquisite packages for senior executives at a major television network.

"We are becoming a global business," Saztec Vice President John Petchel says of the data entry industry.

About 40 U.S. companies have data entry facilities in India, China, South Korea, Mexico, Jamaica, Barbados, and other developing countries, estimates Norman Bodek, president of the Data Entry Management Association in Stamford, Conn.

Although most data entry is still done in the United States, according to a congressional Office of Technology Assessment report released in December, "all signs indicate that offshore data

100

entry could undergo rapid growth over the next 10 to 15 years.''

The developing world offers an attractive labor pool for American entrepreneurs. ''Data entry clerks in Caribbean countries are typically paid about $15 to $60 (U.S.) weekly,'' according to OTA. ''In other countries wages may be much lower.''

While Americans attach little prestige to clerical jobs, workers in low-income developing countries view them as high-status positions. Saztec's data entry operation in the Philippines is made up of workers and managers, nearly all of whom are women with the equivalent of junior college degrees. Turnover is less than 1 percent a year, according to Thomas Reed, Saztec's president.

Because of low labor costs, data entry operations can key information twice and compare the tapes, thus reducing the level of errors. Saztec uses this checking process and guarantees 99.95 percent accuracy.

Hungry for investors, many developing countries offer foreign entrepreneurs tax breaks and lower duties on imports. Jamaica, one of the most aggressive, has successfully encouraged foreign investors to put up a satellite earth station that will provide low-cost, high-quality transmission of information with the United States, says Mark Frazier, president of the Free Zone Authority Ltd., a private Arlington, Va., organization promoting free zone projects.

''Jamaica,'' DEMA's Bodek says, ''is almost making [attraction of data processing entrepreneurs] a national survival issue.''

Because they are so light on their feet, ''information'' industries rapidly create global interdependencies. It takes large amounts of money and time to build steel plants, but only weeks to start up a keypunching operation. Data, unlike iron ore, can be moved in hours.

Saztec stuffs microfilm or documents into bags for shipment by plane; processed information comes back on magnetic tapes or disks.

Moving information by satellites abbreviates the process even more. ''In 20 seconds I can send someone a sheet of paper over satellite,'' Bodek comments. ''It can be keyed and sent back the same day.''

A new Zealander formerly employed by IBM founded Saztec in Singapore in 1970. Saztec set up its headquarters in the United States in 1975.

Saztec has four keypunching facilities in the Philippines. It finds Filipinos particularly good workers, Petchel says, because they have a strong work ethic and strong loyalties.

"There are some companies that have gone offshore and exploited people," Petchel concedes. But Saztec "takes pride that we have brought dollars into a depressed economy."

Reed says Saztec gives Filipino workers a medical program, which includes their family, and paid vacations. Each worker gets profit bonuses based on personal output. Saztec hopes to provide the same benefits to Jamaican workers, he says.

As more companies set up foreign operations in the same region, competition for local workers increases. In northern Mexico, along the U.S. border, firms have started to provide day-care centers for workers' children and free lunches, says Travis Whitlow, promotion manager with A. C. Nielsen. A. C. Nielsen uses Mexicans to count "cents off" coupons that shoppers turn in for discounts on groceries and other consumer products.

The implications of offshore keypunching for American

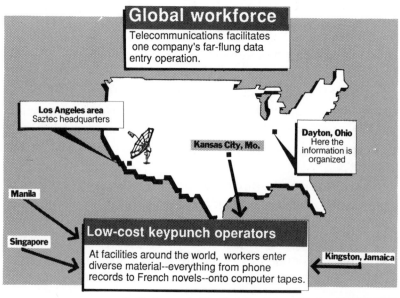

Robin Jareaux in *The Christian Science Monitor* ©1986 TCSPS

workers is uncertain. Vary Coates, an OTA staff member, estimates that only 5,000 to 6,000 American jobs have been lost, and she predicts that automation will make *all* keypunching obsolete eventually. In the meantime, she projects that the number of offshore data entry jobs will increase, forcing American clerical workers to confront adjustment problems sooner.

"There's no way we are going to hang on to data entry," counsels Dr. Stephen Cohen, director of the Berkeley (Calif.) Roundtable on the International Economy. Americans must stay ahead of technological changes and couple these advances with innovative ways of using American workers, he contends.

Further technological advances, observers speculate, could create a wide array of sophisticated international service jobs. "We're not only talking about clerks," says Dennis Chamott, associate director of the AFL-CIO's Department for Professional Employees. "We're talking about engineers, computer programmers, economists, financial analysts, writers, and researchers."

Petchel argues that inexpensive offshore labor makes it possible to expand Saztec's domestic work force. Some companies would not bother computerizing information if Third World data entry costs were not so attractive, he says.

At the same time, Saztec says, it isn't practical to move all keypunching offshore. The firm has a 125-worker facility in Kansas City, Mo., and plans to open another in the United States.

After considering expansion of its keypunching facility in Jamaica, Saztec has decided that local, state, and federal financial incentives make it feasible to put a new facility in an American town. It is looking at sites in Tennessee and Texas.

Saztec plans to train 60 to 100 people initially and hopes eventually to employ 300 in the facility.

Saztec needs domestic keypunching facilities for small jobs and for jobs that require especially quick turnaround or daily communications with the client. Saztec also says that having such a facility means that it can keep its most advanced technology in the United States, a concern of many critics who see offshore activities as a way of exporting American technological advantages.

A U.S. operation is also needed to handle sensitive work for the federal government.

Ironically, Petchel argues, it is often easier to maintain the confidentiality of information when data entry is done overseas. He cites Saztec's keypunching of California telephone numbers, some of which are unlisted.

"Lots of people would like to have telephone numbers of movie stars in Beverly Hills," he says. "Somebody in Manila is not going to call Robert Redford."

**—John Maxwell Hamilton**
*The Christian Science Monitor*
January 27, 1986

# 12

# Third World Ecology: A First World Concern

A TOXIC WASTE DUMP bordering an American community causes chilling fears. Deforestation somewhere in East Africa or Latin America doesn't—but it should.

Environmental problems abroad are American problems.

The consequences of ocean pollution in one part of the world can wash up on our shares, especially as we use the seas more and more as a source of food. The repercussions of an accident in a Third World nuclear power plant, or of improper storage of spent nuclear materials, can spread across national borders, as happened with the nuclear meltdown at Chernobyl. The tragic gas leak at Union Carbide's Bhopal plant has dramatized the moral responsibility that American business can have for human welfare in developing countries—and the consequences multinationals suffer when things go wrong. In the case of Union Carbide, for example, the disaster weakened the company and led to a hostile takeover bid. As a result of strategies to spread risks globally, U.S. insurance companies face massive payments not only for Bhopal but also for natural disasters. "Every country in the world had a piece of the risk in the [1985] Mexico earthquake," says an official at the Risk and Insurance Management Society, with only slight exaggeration.

There is no better example of common U.S.-Third World interests in the environment—and of American failure to recognize them—than in pesticide use. The United States has tough regulations on the use of pesticides domestically that it does not apply to pesticide exports. According to a General Accounting Office report, 29 percent of the pesticides exported in 1976 were not even registered for use in the United States. These pesticides can be especially dangerous for people in developing countries "where literacy and educational levels are lower and where protective equipment and other precautions are absent," comments Jacob Sherr of the Natural Resources Defense Council. They can also hurt Americans. Banned or improperly used pesticides have come back to the United States on food from Mexico and flowers from Colombia. As a result of pesticide residues, according to NRDC's Shelley A. Hearne, "imported foods have twice as many food quality violations as do domestically grown items."[1]

Even if the monitoring of food and flower imports could be made foolproof, Americans would not be fully protected. Third World countries use DDT to kill mosquitoes that carry malaria. Although the United States has outlawed use of the chemical for agricultural purposes—though not for export—it can't stop DDT from coming back from overseas through a combination of wind and rain. "People spray DDT in India, and some of it will wash out in Michigan, Canada, or Bermuda," says Thomas Rohrer, a biologist on the staff of the Michigan Department of Natural Resources.[2]

For residents of developing nations, the effects of relentless deforestation and the steady spread of deserts over once-useful farmland are well documented. "Land degradation and declining rainfall in the region have converted Sudan, one of the world's poorest countries, into a nation of refugee camps and feeding stations," write Lester R. Brown and Edward C. Wolf of the Worldwatch Institute.[3] Notes a World Resources Institute report, "In India alone, the costs of the increasing flood damage and destruction of reservoirs and irrigation systems by sediment

---

1. Shelley A. Hearne, *Harvest of Unknowns: Pesticide Contamination in Imported Foods* (New York: Natural Resources Defense Council, 1984), p. 2.

2. Quoted by Everett G. Martin, *The Wall Street Journal*, May 18, 1985.

3. Lester R. Brown and Edward C. Wolf, "Assessing Ecological Decline," in *State of the World: 1986*, ed. Lester R. Brown and Edward C. Wolf (New York: W. W. Norton, 1986), pp. 27-28.

from misused slopes have averaged $1 billion [in U.S. currency] a year since 1978."[4]

For Americans the consequences are sometimes less obvious but nonetheless real. Deforestation reduces the planet's ability to absorb carbon dioxide in our atmosphere. Destruction of the Panama Canal watershed, brought on by overpopulation, has caused water shortages that restrict passage of ships during certain times of the year. In the case of Haiti, the chain of events set in motion by deforestation—erosion and declining agricultural productivity—created "environmental refugees" flocking to our shores. The leveling of tropical forests in Latin America threatens 90 to 100 species of the U.S. songbirds who winter there. Those birds not only enrich our environments with color and music; they also control pests.

Along with overgrazing and other environmentally unsound practices, deforestation threatens to wipe out exotic flora and fauna, which experts say can have the value of the rosy periwinkle. From that plant, originally found in Madagascar, scientists have produced medicine that gives children an 80 percent chance, rather than the previous 20 percent chance, of surviving leukemia.[5]

The loss of rare germplasm in the Third World is a major threat to the American agricultural base and a good story for any journalist in a farm area. Local universities often have programs to develop improved seeds for locally grown crops. Professors can explain the foreign environmental connections to their work and, as happened in the story below, identify local farmers who understand why environmental problems abroad are American problems.

4. *Tropical Forests: A Call for Action,* Part I, Report of International Task Force convened by the World Resources Institute, the World Bank, and the United Nations Development Programme, 1985, p. 8.

5. Norman Myers, *A Wealth of Wild Species: Storehouse for Human Welfare* (Boulder, Colo.: Westview Press, 1983), pp. 106-107.

# Murdock's Bounty Linked to Germplasm From Third World

MURDOCK, Neb.—Bountiful harvests in the rich Nebraska plains are as American an image as the stars and stripes. The seeds that create those bumper crops fly flags of impoverished Third World countries.

"The majority of the farmers out here," says David Stock, who runs a local seed farm, "don't realize the importance of foreign germplasm," the genetic material used to breed new varieties of high-yielding, disease- and insect-resistant seeds.

Local agronomists who develop the improved varieties of seed that Stock raises are acutely aware of farmers' dependence on germplasm garnered abroad. And they are deeply concerned about conditions in the Third World that could shrink the supply of valuable new genes—among them environmental degradation, inadequate financial resources, and, ironically, the process of development itself.

Whatever blessings American farmland reflects today, the prairies started out poor in food crops. The sunflower is native to the United States. But corn originated in Central America, wheat in the Fertile Crescent, potatoes in the South American Andes, sorghum in Africa, and soybeans in northern China—all countries generally classified as Third World.

Corn spread naturally to North America. Europeans brought wheat with them. The first wheat planting in the colonies is thought to have been at Buzzards Bay, Mass., in the early 17th century.

The continuing process of importing new germplasms and using increasingly sophisticated techniques for crossing them has paid big dividends to farmers here.

Every time a new variety comes in you have a minimum 2 percent to 3 percent increase in yield for just about any crop,"

# Origin of common domestic plants

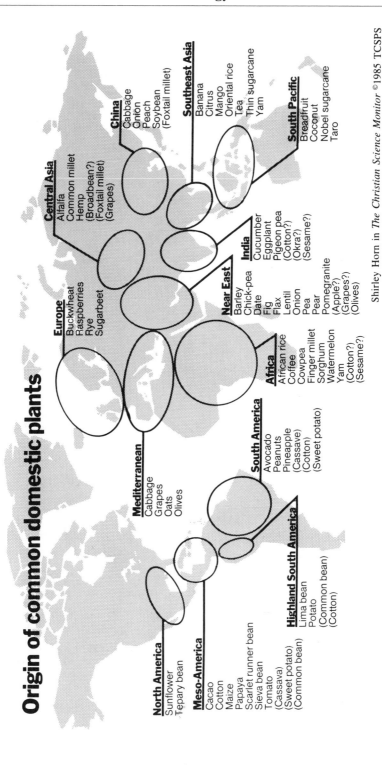

Shirley Horn in *The Christian Science Monitor* ©1985 TCSPS

**Central Asia**
Alfalfa
Common millet
Hemp
(Broadbean?)
(Foxtail millet)
(Grapes)

**China**
Cabbage
Onion
Peach
Soybean
(Foxtail millet)

**Southeast Asia**
Banana
Citrus
Mango
Oriental rice
Tea
Thin sugarcane
Yam

**South Pacific**
Breadfruit
Coconut
Nobel sugarcane
Taro

**Europe**
Buckwheat
Raspberries
Rye
Sugarbeet

**Near East**
Barley
Chick-pea
Date
Fig
Flax
Lentil
Onion
Pea
Pear
Pomegranite
(Apple?)
(Grapes?)
(Olives)

**India**
Cucumber
Eggplant
Pigeon pea
(Cotton?)
(Okra?)
(Sesame?)

**Mediterranean**
Cabbage
Grapes
Oats
Olives

**Africa**
African rice
Coffee
Cowpea
Finger millet
Sorghum
Watermelon
Yam
(Cotton?)
(Sesame?)

**South America**
Avocado
Peanuts
Pineapple
(Cassave)
(Cotton)
(Sweet potato)

**Highland South America**
Lima bean
Potato
(Common bean)
(Cotton)

**North America**
Sunflower
Tepary bean

**Meso-America**
Cacao
Cotton
Maize
Papaya
Scarlet runner bean
Sieva bean
Tomato
(Cassava)
(Sweet potato)
(Common bean)

says Stock, who sells the seed he grows to about 200 farmers and seed dealers.

Because there is scant new land that can be brought into production, improved varieties are the only avenues to bigger harvests. But it is not just the prospects for still bigger harvests that keeps breeders working.

Just as new varieties produce more food for man, they provide "banquet tables" for pests, says Dr. Lee Briggle, who oversees a U.S. Department of Agriculture grain collection facility in Beltsville, Md. To keep ahead of thriving pest populations, farmers must continually introduce varieties with new resistances, sometimes changing crops as often as every four years.

In the search for new germplasm, says Dr. John W. Schmidt, a veteran research agronomist at the University of Nebraska in Lincoln, "the industrialized countries have been pretty well worked over."

Schmidt expects that some of the best new finds will come in the Third World, where isolated communities have sown the same seed for centuries or where wild species have survived.

Among the contributions of Third World germplasm was the discovery at the turn of the century of a Chinese spinach that resisted blight and wilt. In the late 1970s, when a new virus attacked southern U.S. corn crops, researchers developed a resistant variety from a breeding line tracing its ancestry to Cuba.

Breeders use Turkey wheat, a type brought from southern Russia by Mennonites, to produce varieties resistant to stinking bunt, a fungus that attacks crops in the Pacific Northwest and the Great Plains. One additional advantage of Turkey wheat, says Schmidt, is that it has resistance to strip rust, another fungus.

During the 1930s drought, the federal government encouraged the planting of prairie grass in this region to stop erosion. Because native grasses had problems germinating, conservationists used varieties from Central Europe, says Stock, whose great-great-grandparents, German immigrants, homesteaded the land he farms today.

That farmers are not generally aware of the importance of foreign germplasm is not surprising: It can take decades before seed collected on a Turkish hillside or in a village market finds its way into a new variety that is released to farmers.

Schmidt and his colleague of 31 years, Dr. Virgil Johnson, spent more than a decade developing Siouxland wheat, which Stock began to raise last year. This new variety incorporates germplasm originating in a region between the Caspian and Black seas.

Because researchers cannot be sure which germplasm will be useful someday and which won't, they need to collect and preserve every exotic variety possible. "We may not know for 50 years what a plant has, but it may have something," Johnson says.

Finding out a seed variety's precise properties is costly, involving trial plantings in a wide range of settings. But without classification, says Johnson, "the situation is like a drugstore with every shelf full but no labels on the bottles."

Unfortunately, Johnson and Schmidt say, the drugstore is not yet full. In wooden file boxes behind his desk, Johnson has cards for 35,000 varieties of wheat, not quite the total stored in gene banks. Although estimates are sketchy and can differ widely, conservative figures suggest that 10 percent of the cultivated varieties of wheat and 40 percent of the wild varieties have yet to be collected.

Estimates for other crops run much higher. Dr. Judith M. Lyman, a plant scientist at Rutgers University, estimates that gene banks do not have 90 percent of the wild varieties of potatoes, sorghum, runner bean, and cassava.

"There is not a single crop which experts feel we have explored sufficiently," says Johnson.

Collection of additional germplasm has become a race against environmental degradation. Overgrazing by livestock threatens wild wheat species in the Middle East and North Africa. Deforestation has brought on climatic change, which has brought on drought, a process that can kill off species.

The loss of germplasm has environmental implications for the industrialized world, too. Because wild species grow without the help of man, they are especially resistant to insects and disease. Those resistant traits are helpful in breeding varieties that do not require pesticides.

"The loss of genetic diversity, particularly in crop gene pools, may well be the single most serious environmental problem facing mankind,'' according to Dr. Donald L. Plucknett, a World Bank agronomist.

Ironically, economic development improving the lives of farmers in the Third World adds an additional threat to the gene pool. Flooding created behind the Aswan Dam in Egypt is believed to have drowned out unique crop varieties.

"The greatest losses have come when new varieties are introduced," says Johnson of a regular feature of helping farmers raise incomes.

As a Peace Corps volunteer, Stock urged Colombian farmers to use new high-protein corn, for instance. Although he says many resisted, farmers elsewhere have abandoned traditional varieties that have not been preserved. Italian, Greek, and Cypriot farmers switched too quickly to new wheats after World War II. High-yielding Texas hybrids of sorghum now replace most indigenous varieties in South Africa.

"Once lost, it's lost," Johnson says. "You can't go back and get it again."

The USDA and the state of Nebraska fund the work done by Johnson and Schmidt at the university, an international center for breeding red winter wheat. Thirteen internationally funded research centers carry out similar activities in Third World countries, many of which have national programs of their own.

According to a widespread and mounting number of critics, germplasm collection, classification, and preservation suffer because of lack of financial resources. The $55 million spent in 1982—slightly below the level today—is roughly the cost of a single twin-engine Boeing 767, says Plucknett. Much more is spent on breeding, some of which is done by private grain companies such as Cargill.

The USDA currently spends $14.5 million annually on its germplasm program.

"We say to other countries that they should collect the plasm," says Schmidt. "But it is very expensive."

Schmidt and Johnson visited a Turkish experimental agricultural station several years ago, where the electricity was turned off a couple of days each week because of budgetary problems.

Seed preservation requires constant refrigeration.

Third World countries have little problem acquiring seed developed by international centers or the USDA. But they must pay for privately developed seed, which has provoked North-South acrimony.

Contending that it is "genetic imperialism" for companies to collect germplasm freely in their countries and sell the improved varieties back to them, some developing nations say the entire international seed system should be revamped. Some Third World member countries supported such proposals at a Food and Agriculture Organization biannual conference in Rome last month.

One bright spot in North-South cooperation is improved U.S.-Chinese relations, which has given breeders access to new soybean germplasm. The payoff in higher yields could come at the end of the century, says Stock, who is also an official with the American Soybean Association.

Researchers are meanwhile considering ways of introducing new Third World crops into the United States. If they succeed, amaranth, grown by the Aztecs, and quinoa, raised by the Incas, may someday flourish in the fields around Murdock.

**—John Maxwell Hamilton**
*The Christian Science Monitor*
December 2, 1985

# 13

# When the Third World Sneezes . . .

*Swords and lances, arrows, machine guns, and even high explosives have had far less power over the fates of the nations than the typhus louse, the plague flea, and the yellow-fever mosquito.* —Hans Zinsser[1]

*In the era in which we live, there is no infectious disease endemic in one part of the world that may not appear in another.* —Myron G. Schultz[2]

THE HISTORY OF CIVILIZATION is marked by the wanderings of diseases. Smallpox, for example. Europeans brought smallpox to the New World. It was a major ally in defeating native Americans. Hans Zinsser has also suggested that a smallpox outbreak prevented the Carthaginians from overtaking the nascent Roman Empire, thus setting back the development of global commerce.

Modern advances have armed the world to fight human diseases as well as agricultural pests. Interdependence has made it all the more important for Americans to understand their stake in eradicating Third World ailments.

Local connections to Third World diseases are routine. An old saw about U.S. economic power has it that when the United States sneezes, Latin America catches cold. Looked at literally,

---

1. Hans Zinsser, *Rats, Lice and History* (Boston: Little, Brown, 1934), p. 9.

2. Myron G. Schultz, "Unde Venis? (Where Have You Been?)," *Journal of the American Medical Association* 251 (January 27, 1984): p. 513.

however, when people in developing countries sneeze, Americans catch the flu. All major U.S. flu epidemics have originated abroad, mostly in developing countries. The devastating Russian flu in 1977, in fact, started in China. Researchers traced the three flu strains circulating in the United States in early 1986 to the Philippines, China, and the Soviet Union.

At one time, foreign travel to developing countries was arduous, often fatal. Dr. David Livingstone died of dysentery in search of the headwaters of the Nile. And although Abercrombie & Kent, a Chicago tour operator, arranges Kenya safaris complete with "luxury tent suites," there are still risks. Several years ago, 15 of 18 teenagers visiting Kenya contracted schistosomiasis, a parasitic disease caused by blood flukes, apparently from swimming. Travelers can return home with other parasites or malaria.

European agricultural pests have troubled Americans for centuries. We still fight Hessian flies, which arrived during the Revolutionary War in the straw bedding of German mercenaries. Together with wheat stem rust, which came on barberry plants from Europe, the flies devastated U.S. wheat crops during World War I.

Commerce with the developing world more recently brought the khapra beetle, which has destroyed grain from New Jersey to Texas. The alfalfa weevil, from southern Europe and the Middle East, is a nationwide problem. Exotic New Castle disease, which infects chickens, came on partridges and pheasants from Hong Kong in 1950.

The cause of Third World diseases and pests—and the clue to how industrialized nations can cope with them—lies in poverty, which leaves people defenseless. Third World statistics tell the grim story: Low-income developing countries average one physician for about every 6,000 people. In the industrialized world, the ratio is 1-to-550. One in 10 babies in those developing countries dies before reaching one year of age, as opposed to one in 100 in industrialized countries.[3] "Four-fifths of the rural populations of 73 African and Asian countries do not have access

---

3. The World Bank, *The World Tables II* (Baltimore, Md.: John Hopkins University Press, 1983), pp. 158-159.

to clean drinking water," according to William Chandler.[4]

With scant financial resources, developing countries find it difficult not only to treat diseases or eradicate pests but also to identify them promptly. In a story examining the possibility that Acquired Immune Deficiency Syndrome originated in Africa, *Los Angeles Times* medical reporter Harry Nelson describes the problem: "AIDS, many researchers believe, may be a classic example of what can emerge from the caldron of disease-causing organisms...that infect hundreds of millions of people in the Third World....[And] in countries where medical systems are underdeveloped, malnutrition is common, infectious diseases rampant and sophisticated diagnostic services nonexistent, even AIDS could have passed unnoticed for an indefinite period, researchers say."[5]

Cures for Third World ailments can make a big difference to citizens of industrialized nations. Dr. Myron Schultz, of the Center for Disease Control, points especially to the eradication of smallpox: "In 1968, smallpox-related activities [such as vaccinations and quarantine activities] cost the U.S. Government $150 million [annually]. The cost of U.S. support for the WHO [World Health Organization] smallpox programme and the bilateral programme with 19 West African countries was [about $ 9 million annually]. Now neither expense is necessary."[6]

Journalists can write stories on these themes locally. Harry Nelson's article, for example, does not have a foreign dateline. The U.S. Department of Agriculture's Animal and Plant Health Inspection Service (APHIS) has eight regional offices in the United States plus numerous other laboratories and research stations that deal with plant and animal pests. The article below looks at citrus canker, an agricultural pest in Florida.

---

4. William Chandler, "Investing in Children," in *State of the World: 1986*, ed. Lester R. Brown and Edward C. Wolf (New York: W. W. Norton, 1986), pp. 167-168.

5. Harry Nelson, *Los Angeles Times*, February 22, 1985.

6. M. G. Schultz, "The Forgotten Problems of Forgotten People," in *Health Policies in Developing Countries*, Royal Society of Medicine International Congress and Symposium Series, no. 24 (London: Academic Press Inc. and Royal Society of Medicine, n.d.), pp. 57-62.

# Winter Haven Battles Citrus Canker

WINTER HAVEN, Fla.—In September, Bill Adams' 60-acre citrus nursery, the largest in the state, became a wasteland of sandy soil punctuated by small piles of burning brush.

Adams' nursery is one of many battlefronts where Florida and the federal government are fighting citrus canker, a mysterious bacteria most experts believe originated in the Third World. To control the quickly spreading bacteria, officials have ordered on-sight burning of affected nurseries, even if only a few infected trees are found.

The battle also involves efforts to find the bacteria's geographic origin, to establish an effective quarantine, and, if possible, to support eradication efforts abroad.

So far the problem has been confined to nurseries, not functioning citrus groves, and there is no evidence that it has spread beyond Florida. But scientists have been unable to identify the variety of bacteria that has threatened the state's $2.5 billion-a-year citrus industry since last fall.

Since the first sighting in August 1984, 13 Florida nurseries containing more than 11 million trees have gone up in smoke. In recent days, officials have found evidence of the bacteria in two additional nurseries—the most recent confirmed on Saturday—and in two groves not yet in production, where destruction will not be as extensive but will still be costly to growers.

Working together, the USDA and the Florida Department of Agriculture and Consumer Services must also find and destroy about 1.5 million trees sold by the affected nurseries to groves, retail outlets, and other nurseries.

Meanwhile, a constant cycle of inspections—including examination of some three million trees at private residences—continues in hopes of locating other infections before they spread.

Citrus canker causes brown lesions on twigs and leaves, which can defoliate and kill trees. Corky brown blemishes appear on oranges, grapefruit, and other fruit, making them susceptible to rotting and unmarketable as fresh produce.

One problem in figuring out how to keep the canker out of groves, where it has not yet been found, lies in determining how it arrived in Florida in the first place. "We need a good detective," says Charles O. Youtsey, who directs a state-operated arboretum selling propagative materials to citrus growers.

By process of elimination, USDA officials trace the "Florida strain" of citrus canker, as the new variety is called, to somewhere in the Third World—most likely East Asia, where citrus trees originated. Other types of canker exist throughout Latin America, including Mexico, where a different strain currently afflicts limes.

With scientists only able to guess how the canker actually entered Florida, theories abound, ranging from sabotage to innocent accident. A scenario for the latter and more likely possibility could be as simple as a nursery worker visiting an infected farm in a developing country and bringing the bacteria home on his tools.

The canker could also have come from contaminated fruit or root stock imported or smuggled into the United States. Although USDA's Animal and Plant Health Inspection Service tries to keep contaminated materials out of the country, it is difficult to spot travelers bringing in small items, such as citrus leaves used to make tea.

The mystery of where the Florida strain originated is especially perplexing because the problem was first discovered in a nursery owned by Franklyn Ward, regarded as one of the most reputable and careful men in the Florida citrus business. "Why me and not some fly-by-night operation?" asks the baffled nurseryman, who wonders if the cause may not be some genetic mutation.

Citrus canker is only one of several Florida agricultural problems originating in the Third World. Fruit flies, probably from Latin America, have come in three times in this decade. Red wax scale from the Caribbean has infected foliage nurseries near here.

118

In the 1960s APHIS eradicated the Giant African Snail from the state.

Similar agricultural insects and diseases from the Third World can be found in every part of the United States. Last year, the corn cyst nematode, previously found only in India, Pakistan, and Egypt, showed up in the United States for the first time. The nematode eats the roots of several major food crops.

This year USDA quarantined part of California to prevent the spread of Africanized honeybees, so-called killer bees, from Brazil.

Although the Third World is not the only source of pests, these low-income developing nations pose special hazards. Americans have learned to live with many European plant diseases introduced by immigrants before USDA quarantine laws were put in place at the beginning of the century, says Dr. Stephen Poe, a USDA plant pathologist working on the Florida citrus canker problem.

Today, he says, "Third World immigrants—and increased trade with the Third World—bring in new diseases."

USDA helps developing countries eradicate pests before they leave their borders, but this often proves difficult.

American consumers are particular about the appearance of fruit and vegetables and will leave those with the slightest blemish in grocery bins. Third World consumers are not so finicky, and growers in those countries are therefore not quick to notice marks that might signal disease or insects.

Third World countries have themselves made major contributions to efforts to counter diseases like citrus canker. Argentina developed a defoliation technique that can be used to control the spread of citrus canker in groves.

Even so, governments in the developing world typically don't have the resources to fight diseases, says Poe, who has worked on the Mexican citrus canker problem. Third World government officials often concede that they cannot undertake control programs because the economic disruption would cause political protests, he says.

"Agricultural systems in the Third World are not buffered the way we are," says Poe, noting that the USDA and the Florida

119

government are partially reimbursing citrus growers, most of whom have sufficient capital to withstand setbacks.

Government costs have already reached $28 million, says Gordon Johnson, deputy director of the 850-member joint USDA-Florida Agriculture Department staff working on the problem. He figures that the program will run an additional three years.

The job is particularly challenging because the goal is to wipe out citrus canker, not simply to control it.

Measures include a prohibition on all interstate shipments of citrus plants and on sales of fruit to other citrus-growing states. Packers must observe strict procedures to disinfect fruit before shipment to non-citrus growing states.

The USDA-Florida reimbursement program for nurseries and growers has not offset their losses. Franklyn Ward, whose nursery was the first hit, estimates he has lost about $400,000.

Estimates of total losses to the Florida citrus industry are difficult "because we don't know all the implications yet," says Ernie Neff of Florida Citrus Mutual, an association representing growers.

One study, he says, conservatively estimates that it costs growers, packers, and processors at least $14 million annually to comply with sanitary regulations. Ultimately, all or part of those costs will be passed along to American consumers as higher prices for fresh citrus.

In addition, the citrus canker problem has created a scarcity of new trees. This comes at a time when growers need to replace one-quarter of their groves because of killing freezes during four of the last five years.

The loss of production will cost millions, according to Neff.

Government rules forbid a nursery from resuming operation for one year after canker is discovered. Ward, whose father helped pioneer the citrus industry in Florida, worries that growers will be wary of buying from him after he starts his operation again. "People will say, 'I like the guy, but I have to think of myself' and go elsewhere," Ward says.

USDA officials say it is likely they will find the citrus problem at other nurseries and eventually groves. If they succeed in eradicating canker, however, it won't be the first time.

Citrus canker infested Florida in 1914 and spread to other citrus states before it was eradicated in 1933. An estimated 20 million trees were destroyed.

—**John Maxwell Hamilton**
*The Christian Science Monitor*
October 7, 1985

# 14

# Global Drug Addiction

LOOK AT THE DRUG PROBLEM in any American high school and you'll get a perspective on underdevelopment abroad.

The major illegal drug-producing areas are in developing countries. Opium comes from the Golden Triangle region of Southeast Asia, from the Golden Crescent in the Middle East and South Asia, and from Mexico. Coca leaves to make cocaine come from Latin America, particularly the Andean region. Latin America and the Caribbean account for most of the marijuana smuggled into the United States.

The one thing these countries have in common is large numbers of poor farmers, desperate for cash crops.

A senior Bolivian official explained to a reporter from *The Washington Post* how it all fits together: "This is a transnational problem. On the one hand, there is the superdevelopment of the United States, which encourages exaggerated consumption; on the other, there is our own underdevelopment, which induces the peasant into producing this drug. No program of crop substitution will work in which the peasants earn less than they do from coca."

Mike Ward, an investigative reporter with *The Tulsa Tribune*, pieced the story together for his readers without visiting the steaming jungles of South America. He did make a call to the U.S. Embassy in Bogota, Colombia. But it wasn't necessary, he said. He got better information from local sources, from the U.S. Attorney's office and Drug Enforcement Administration officials, and with calls to the State Department's Bureau of International Narcotics Matters and to an Oklahoma congressman who follows drug issues. Ward used "The International Narcotics Control Strategy Report," which the State Department submits annually to Congress. The report gives details on foreign drug production.

# Drug Problems In Tulsa Start In Latin America

TULSA, Okla.—Tulsa U.S. Attorney Layn Phillips said that to stop the influx of cocaine, two types of addicts must be cured:

One is a user in America, where the craving for the illicit $100-a-gram whitish stimulant sustains a web of crime.

The other is a number of Third World countries in the Caribbean or South and Central America, where dependence on the dollars paid for cocaine has warped and corrupted economies.

The countries' habit, according to federal officials in Washington, is at the center of a growing crisis in international diplomacy and finance.

"Every time someone in Tulsa buys a $100 bag of cocaine, he contributes to the warp," Phillips said. "South American farmers grow coca leaves because they can make money doing it. Because the economies are so bad that cash keeps the governments afloat.

"But if there was no market for the drugs—if people in Tulsa and elsewhere weren't using cocaine—those farmers wouldn't be growing those coca leaves."

Budget belt-tightening in Washington is expected to shrink anti-drug aid to South American countries and trim U.S. drug-interdiction efforts.

The result, Washington and Oklahoma officials warn, could be more drugs for local lawmen to deal with.

U.S. Rep. Glenn English, the Oklahoma Democrat who heads a House subcommittee that oversees enforcement against drug smuggling, said the problem has developed into a "vicious circle."

"The economies of some countries have become dependent upon the drug trade. If that is stopped, their economy collapses, they can't repay their [foreign bank] loans, and some big U.S. banks will then be in trouble," said English, D-6th District.

English and Phillips said the drug problem used to be dealt with from a local perspective: Police put pushers and users in jail and considered the problem solved.

"We're beginning to see the bigger problems from drugs," English said.

"There's no easy solution."

State Department and federal Drug Enforcement Administration officials said the problem has worsened in recent years as the world economy has worsened.

Highly affected are a number of countries—such as Colombia, Jamaica, Peru, Ecuador, and Bolivia—all plagued by foreign debt problems and economic stagnation, which have made it even more difficult for poor farmers to feed their families.

Phillips said recent cocaine busts in Tulsa highlight the international problems to which Tulsa drug users contribute.

Smugglers bring the cocaine into the United States from Colombia and Peru, he said, where it is processed from raw coca leaves. About one-half of the leaves come from Bolivia, where they are grown by native farmers, according to DEA and State Department reports.

The people of that small Andean nation have the lowest per capita income in South America, about $410 a year. The farmers—called campesinos—sell coca leaves to middlemen who move the cargo to refiners.

DEA reports show that refineries in the Bolivian jungle pay about $1200 for 200 kilograms—about 440 pounds—of coca leaves.

In Tulsa, Phillips said, a single kilo of refined cocaine will bring $50,000 to $60,000. Middlemen and smugglers share in those whopping profits.

"Coca leaf production is virtually the only bright spot in the

Bolivian economy,'' said Larry Deaton, a Department of Agriculture economist in Washington studying the drug crop problem.

''Control of that crop is made especially difficult by the instability of the Bolivian political system and the harsh realities facing the Bolivian economy.''

Bolivia has changed governments an average of more than once a year since it gained independence in 1825. In the past four years, its economy has deteriorated steadily because of droughts, floods, declining mineral prices, and the worldwide recession.

For the past two years, its annual inflation rate has topped 1,500 percent.

That has left the Bolivian treasury depleted and government officials under pressure to repay a $2.5 billion debt to world lenders—including the International Monetary Fund and several big U.S. banks.

Because coca is a major cash producer, English said, government officials have been reluctant to crack down.

That reluctance has been heightened, State Department officials said, because many of those who pay poor campesinos to grow coca leaves are well connected politically. These farmers constitute a huge political majority in many rural areas.

In addition, laws—some in Peru date back to the 16th century—legalize coca leaf production for medicines and flavorings.

U.S. pressure to eradicate the Bolivian coca crop—including threats to cut off foreign aid or block further IMF loans—has drawn a backlash.

A recent Bolivian crackdown left government troops encircled for several days by heavily armed campesinos, who realized their livelihood was threatened. According to news reports, a major coca entrepreneur provided the arms.

Officials said the troops eventually departed, leaving the coca crops untouched.

Under a U.S. aid program, the Bolivian government has offered a one-time, $1400-an-acre payment to farmers who stop growing coca. Most have refused, they note, because an acre of coca can yield $4,000 a year.

"The drug problem and economic situation are very ticklish issues," a State Department spokesman said.

The United States wants drugs stopped. But we can't demand the impossible when the realities of a country won't allow it."

In the early 1970s, Turkey acted under U.S. pressure to eradicate its heroin production with strict new laws and harsh enforcement.

The result, DEA officials said, virtually dried up Turkey as a major supply point.

But they acknowledge that the problems in Bolivia and its neighbors are more complex, involving economic as well as administrative difficulties.

Deaton said that because coca brings in more cash than food crops, many peasants have given up commercial farming.

"When farmers plant coca instead of corn, the victims are not only drug users but also hungry children in the highlands of Bolivia and elsewhere," Deaton said.

Because U.S. demand for cocaine has increased coca production, DEA officials and English said, the supply sources have become almost unlimited.

If one supplier is shut down or arrested, they said, several others can quickly take his place.

Economic and political development—including higher prices for Bolivian food crops and an end to government corruption—is often cited as a way to cut back coca production.

Another solution lies in Tulsa, Phillips said.

"The root of the problem. . . is the person. . . buying the cocaine. If there wasn't such a demand for it here, those farmers wouldn't have anyone to sell to.

"We wouldn't have the problem with addicts—here or there."

—**Mike Ward**
*The Tulsa Tribune*
February 7, 1986

# 15_____

# Immigrants: Why They Come, What They Bring

*"As a nation built by waves of immigrants from colonial times to the present, we know remarkably little about the composition and characteristics of the flow of new arrivals in any given year or about how they settle in to their new lives in the United States."*—Immigration Statistics: A Story of Neglect[1]

IMMIGRATION FROM DEVELOPING COUNTRIES confronts Americans with serious public policy questions. Are immigrants an "economic asset" or do they displace American workers?[2] How much does our balance of payments deteriorate because immigrants send money to relatives who are not able to get into the United States? What demands do refugees fleeing political upheavals in Southeast Asia put on social services? What steps will be most effective in stopping illegal immigration from Mexico: more patrols along the border or, as Sen. Paul Simon of Illinois has suggested, long-term cooperation with the Mexican government to better the Mexican economy?

Journalists cannot improve Immigration and Naturalization Service record keeping, criticized in the report cited above, *Immigration Statistics*. They can, however, look at immigrants in their own community to help answer some of the questions that statistics

---

1. Report of the National Research Council Panel on Immigration Statistics, ed. David B. Levine, Kenneth Hill, and Robert Warren (Washington, D.C.: National Academy Press, 1985), p. 2.

2. Quoted from Rand report, "Mexican Immigration into California: Current and Future Effects," in *The New York Times*, December 12, 1985.

address. By doing that, reporters also provide a rich array of information on life in the Third World.

As indicated by the list of sources in Appendix One, a wide range of national organizations follow immigration issues. Specialized groups often do their own studies. As an example, the National Science Foundation monitors the annual inflows of scientists and engineers. Census data provide local counts of foreign-born residents. And reporters can turn to churches and other local human service organizations for help.

When the Middletown, N.Y., *Times Herald-Record* assigned Rita Giordano to look at Third World immigrants in the mid-Hudson region, she met newcomers by volunteering to help teach English as a second language at the public high school. Her wide contacts put her in touch with illegal immigrants from Mexico, a Chilean who immigrated in search of "the riches to be had in America," an Ethiopian who sought relief from the political problems in his homeland, and a Cambodian refugee, the subject of the piece below.

The Middletown newspaper is an Ottaway newspaper. To tie Giordano's vignettes together, Mark Gruenberg at the Ottaway bureau in Washington, D.C., wrote a three-part series summarizing the region's economic ties to the developing world. The entire package ran for over three days in January 1986. Summing up her experience on the series, Giordano said afterward, "It was a high, seeing something you never saw before."

The second story reprinted below appeared in *The Hopewell* (Va.) *News*. Aware that the community had attracted large numbers of foreign doctors, editor Kathryn C. Weigel asked reporter Missy Epps and assistant editor Henry Sharber to find out why. Their chief problem was convincing local Third World doctors to release information about themselves. After Ms. Weigel met with a group of physicians at the local hospital, they agreed to cooperate. She "gave them a Hopewell history lesson," explaining that Hopewell had a long tradition of welcoming immigrants. She later summed up the feeling in an editorial: "This special group of physicians has enriched our community and our lives medically, culturally and, perhaps most importantly, humanly. Our world and the Third World are one."

# Cambodian Finds New Life In Newburgh

NEWBURGH, N.Y.—"Life is wonderful, life is great," Vuol Kim says. He laughs often, almost giggles, in a voice as soft as a Cambodian mountain dawn.

It has been years since Kim woke to such a dawn. He seems at ease with his recently found American way. His desk-long blaster fills his college dorm room with Billy Joel songs. His laundry chugs toward weekend readiness in a machine downstairs.

Kim, only 20, found his way across the world to a dorm room at Mount St. Mary's College. He did it alone.

Cambodia, Thailand, Singapore, Hong Kong, San Francisco, Dallas, New York. Whisked along the refugee-relief route like a leaf in wind.

He laughs at that. He laughs, too, with the lightness of his good fortune, a paid education, a future.

But what about the past? What about his life in Cambodia, in the war?

Kim's smile leaves. His dark eyes look wary. They don't blink.

He mentions a mother, siblings.

The time is about six years ago. He pleads poor memory. "When my mother leave, I don't remember. . ."

Did he go with his family?

"No."

Was it because he was the oldest?

No, in fact, he was the youngest.

"Excuse me, I have to check the laundry."

Kim comes back, his smile regained.

What did he do when he got to New York City?

"I call a taxi," he teases.

What did he do when his family left Cambodia?

The smile leaves, the wary look returns. He mentions being in the army, fighting the communists.

But he couldn't have been more than 14. "Fourteen, 13, 12, they don't care." And it was a way to get a weapon. He slept with his weapon.

His hand slips to his right hip. He mentions wounds.

He says his mother wanted him to flee with the family to Vietnam. But Vietnam is communist, too. "I think it better to find the freedom."

"I said, 'No, Mom, I don't want to go. Bye-bye, Mom.' " His voice is as soft as the child he was then. "She crying, she sad. 'Mom, bye-bye.' "

After his family left, he stayed in the jungle, sometimes with the other fighters, sometimes alone. Sometimes the enemy was Cambodian, sometimes Vietnamese.

Many other people stayed in the jungle, too, trying to stay alive. He describes swallowing gold, slipping into Thailand, defecating the gold, and using it to buy food, cloth.

"It was war." He talks fast. His eyes burn, his mouth wavers between the borders of rage and tears.

"You could not grow anything." Too quickly it became shooting ground. "You couldn't go to buy food. They shot you."

Kim pulls two articles from a drawer. This, he says, grasping a dull blue roll of cloth wrapped with cord, is the hammock that was his jungle bed. The other is the pelt of a rabbit he killed for food. He says he showed it once to a girl here; it frightened her.

He talks about evading the communist soldiers. When you saw them, he says, you could tell if they were about to kill by their eyes. He makes those eyes—vibrating eyes, like an animal crazed with the scent of blood.

"My idea was to get a weapon and escape. When you have a weapon," he whispers, "you can do anything."

His eyes become like the soldiers. Just for an instant. Then there is sadness.

Again, his hand goes to his wound. He was crossing the Thai border, back into the Cambodian jungle, he says. He was carrying food, precious food. Someone saw him. Then someone threw a grenade.

To kill him for food?

"Yes." The word comes out like a muffled cry.

"There is no discipline." Soldiers kill soldiers, soldiers kill people, people kill each other. "You can kill *anybody*."

"Life has no meaning. Here life has meaning."

Kim is quiet. Softly, he tells of the final trek into Thailand, to a refugee camp. The word "father" for the first time slips from his lips.

He tells how "they"—the communists—do not like people who associate with Americans. "They put fabric over their eyes." His eyes seem veiled.

"They let the people watch. . ."

He is describing the public execution of his father.

No, he continues, he was not there to see. His voice will remain soft. He says his mother wrote him about his father's death while he was in Thailand.

They have corresponded since. She wrote that the communists are teaching her Russian. He wants to bring her here. Other Southeast Asian families have let their children come here through relief agencies with the hope the youngsters will be able to bring the rest of the family over.

But Kim's mother is afraid to risk the escape from Vietnam. Kim says he understands the fear.

The last time she wrote was last year. Kim says he has not written back. She did not say she needed food, but he says he can read behind her words. He is afraid that if he keeps in touch, he will quit college and throw away his future for work that will give him money to help her now.

His tuition, room, and board is paid through government-student assistance and the state-funded Higher Education Opportunity Program. He knows the students in his dorm and says people are good to him. He knows adults in the community who, from time to time, fill in for the family he has left behind.

But he concentrates on his studies and wants to do well in the land he has adopted. Soon, he will start a work-study job at the college library—a place already familiar.

Sometimes, though, he says he has troubled sleep. Once, he woke up crying, speaking the language of his people. Last Fourth of July, fireworks woke him and sent him grasping for a weapon.

What he wants, he says, is to study for the medical profession, the profession of healing.

"Life is wonderful," he says. Slightly, he smiles. "Life is great..."

—**Rita Giordano**
*Times Herald-Record*
January 14, 1986

# Third World Doctors Heal In Hopewell

HOPEWELL, Va.—Remember the Norman Rockwell painting of the country doctor and his youthful patient? There are still some of those Anglo-Saxon country doctors around Hopewell, but the face of the medical profession has been changing.

In the last decade and a half, an influx of foreign-born and foreign-educated physicians has filled local medical ranks with specialists from diverse ethnic and cultural backgrounds.

The homelands of the physicians who came to this small industrial city and other American communities during the 1970s appear as datelines on stories that seem remote and unimportant to many Americans.

But experts and the physicians themselves say events and conditions in places like Manila, Bhopal, and Taipei are important reasons doctors came to America.

The impact on the medical services available in Hopewell is significant.

Thirty-two of the 67 members of John Randolph Hospital's medical staff are from Third World countries. Nine come from the Philippines, eight from India, seven from Taiwan, three from Thailand, two from Korea, and one each from Malaysia, Kenya, and Indonesia.

"The whole thing is tied to the political and social climate," said Dr. Bernard Logan, assistant professor of geography at Old Dominion University. Logan said his research on the migration of professionals shows two primary reasons for physicians leaving their Third World homes: to make a better living and to have better research facilities.

"There isn't the opportunity [to make a good living] in developing countries because they have a poorer standard of living. That's the perception even if it is false," said Logan, who is originally from the West African nation of Sierra Leone. "They feel they will improve their families' standard of living by coming here."

Dr. Virgilio C. "Bill" Supetran, who specializes in obstetrics and gynecology, came to the United States from the Philippines for what he considered a better way of life and a better quality of medicine.

American medicine, he said, is the best in the world. "You get used to the program here [and it is] very hard to go back to where you came from."

Supetran arrived in Hopewell in 1973, shortly after the John Randolph Hospital administration and Hopewell Hospital Authority began recruiting physicians.

In the early 1970s JRH, which serves about 80,000 people, needed to expand. "We had somewhere between 15 and 20 physicians on our staff," said Hopewell Hospital Authority member George E. Spatig Jr. And the staff was growing older, with an average age of 48.

"We had to do something to be progressive. We just couldn't stand still and not improve our facilities," he added.

Homer B. Thomas Sr., also a member of the authority, said that it was all "part of strategic and long-range planning....We needed to do something as far as specialists were concerned to keep the citizens from having to go to MCV [the Medical Col-

## Selected Medical Statistics

| | Population | Hospital Beds (per 100,000 population) | Physicians (per 100,000 population) |
|---|---|---|---|
| India | 730,572,000 | 75 | 26 |
| Indonesia | 165,787,000 | 60 | 7 |
| Kenya | 18,580 | 128 | 8 |
| South Korea | 41,366,000 | 68 | 49 |
| Malaysia | 14,995,000 | 308 | 12 |
| Philippines | 54,252,000 | 162 | 81 |
| Taiwan | 18,786,000 | 143 | 111 |
| Thailand | 50,731,000 | 121 | 12 |
| United Kingdom | 56,009,000 | 894 | 153 |
| United States | 234,249,000 | 555 | 176 |
| Virginia | 5,346,797 | 366 | 205 |

Source: Newspaper Enterprise Association's "World Almanac & Book of Facts"

*The Hopewell* (Va.) *News*

lege of Virginia Hospitals in Richmond] and other hospitals.''

After the decision had been made to recruit doctors, the authority turned to a statewide organization, the Virginia Council on Health and Medical Care, for aid. The referral service, which assisted other communities in the state to recruit doctors, was provided to the hospital without cost.

''They would send out a monthly questionnaire to all the hospitals saying, are you looking for doctors and, if you are, what type of doctors are you looking for?'' said Franklin D. Boyce, JRH chief executive officer. ''Here at John Randolph Hospital we were looking for an obstetrician, a cardiologist, and an orthopedic surgeon.''

''We didn't look specifically for foreign doctors,'' Boyce said. ''It really never occurred to any of us, the medical staff or the authority, to concern ourselves with the fact that the doctors were foreign-trained [or] from another country. We were looking at their specialties. . . [and] their qualifications.''

The market for foreign physicians in the United States has grown since World War II. Nearly 100,000 foreign-born doctors are practicing in the United States today, a number that is up 40 percent in the past 10 years, *The Wall Street Journal* has reported.

The same growth market hasn't existed in Third World

nations, even though the people of those countries need more medical care, Logan said.

"I don't think that any Third World country can claim that they have enough doctors. But there just isn't a place [for them to practice]. There are only so many hospitals and clinics. The economy [in those countries] is not expanding fast enough [to support the extra doctors]," Logan said.

Doctors who study in First World or industrialized countries, he added, have high expectations about research facilities. They get used to the way it is done in the West; "then they go home and see the corrupt politicians and realize that the government will never spend money on the research."

Baljit and Jatinder Sidhu are married physicians from India who came to the United States in 1977 and moved to Hopewell in 1981, prompted by the chance for a better living and more education.

"People that go out into a different country. . . stand a better chance, like in the United States or Europe or Canada," Baljit Sidhu said. "They feel they have a better opportunity to further their cause, to further their knowledge and make a living."

There are plenty of patients for doctors in the Philippines, said OB-GYN specialist Supetran, but most of them cannot afford to buy medicine, and that interferes with the doctor's ability to have the type of practice he or she wants.

Dr. Yi-Nan Chou, an internal medicine and cardiovascular disease specialist born in Taiwan, originally came to the United States in 1968 for further training. He believes it's "more fun to practice" medicine in the United States. "I think this [is] a free country."

Jatinder Sidhu, a physician who lived in England before coming to the United States with her husband, had an additional reason for immigrating. She wanted to escape the prejudices that existed in England against Indians.

The British, she said, are nice "if you just take people for their face value. . . . But I think the prejudices go a long way because they ruled Indians for so many years."

At first Jatinder Sidhu expected to go back to India, but a different type of prejudice existed there. "Once we had our son. . .

I had become so independent, and the customs over there [in India required]...that [women] be dependent.''

A medical practice in the United States was the answer. She is one of nine women on the JRH staff. Six of them are foreign-born.

''We knew that we had a lot of opportunity here. I wanted to specialize and my husband was going through specialization,'' Jatinder Sidhu said. ''Once you get used to all the luxuries of having a CAT scanner and a good lab,...not having all that would be difficult to get adjusted to.''

For her husband, becoming a physician was a way to escape the agrarian life of his native Punjab region of India. ''I come from a family of farmers,'' he said. ''My whole family does nothing but agriculture.''

JRH has changed dramatically in the past several years. The staff has grown to 67 physicians with specialties in about 23 areas. A CAT scanner, a mammography suite to aid in the detection of breast cancer, nuclear technology, a larger radiology department, and a progressive care unit are among the advanced facilities that have been added.

Last June the hospital opened a surgery floor, an intensive and coronary care unit, and a variety of office and waiting room spaces.

The influx of physicians into the Hopewell area accounts for much of that growth and success at JRH, said hospital administration and Hopewell Hospital Authority members. But academicians and some of the doctors are concerned about the effects of this immigration on the developing countries.

''We get the benefit without having to pay the cost of training,'' said Dr. Christine Drake, an associate professor specializing in Third World issues at Old Dominion University.

This is part of the ''brain drain'' theory, said Drake, used to describe the process by which highly educated and talented people leave the Third World, which ''desperately needs them.''

Several countries are trying to stop this drain, she said, by levying exit taxes, making professionals work in the country for a set period, or making them pay back money used for schooling.

But some countries such as India, Drake said, don't have

enough jobs to provide employment for the number of professionals there. One of the reasons that doctors do not stay, she added, is low wages.

"There are more than enough physicians for the jobs provided by the government," Baljit Sidhu said. "For 10 jobs that are advertised there are more than 100 applicants looking for that job."

Logan argues that the physicians' exit is a "relief" to Third World countries in some ways. It reduces unemployment, and some of the physicians who find good-paying practices in the United States begin sending money back to their families.

Regardless of the reasons why physicians leave Third World countries—or the consequences—the result is a well-qualified medical staff in Hopewell, Boyce said.

And it's a unified staff, Boyce said. "When we see our doctors here, we don't see foreign doctors."

"When I call up Dr. Chou..., it never crosses my mind that Dr. Chou is not from the United States," Boyce said. Chou and others "are medical staff members and are treated exactly like everyone else and they treat us exactly like everyone else.... They are one of us."

—**Missy Epps and Henry Sharber**
*The Hopewell News*
March 13, 1986

# 16

# A Taste of Third World Culture

CULTURE, that amorphous concept that embraces everything from the cut of our clothes to the way we think about the universe, defines a society. Inevitably, Third World influences are redefining ours.

Consider:

—*Travel.* Americans are traveling more and more to developing countries. The Third World is more accessible and more economical, and it holds special charms—for example, wilder rapids for the canoeist or simply a different way of life for those who want to get away from it all. Statistics compiled by the U.S. Travel and Tourism Administration show that American travel to South America was up 6 percent from the previous year in 1983 and up 15 percent more in 1984. Statistics for the first half of 1984 showed that less than one-half of all travel abroad was to Europe. Mary Anne Weeks of Travel Unlimited in Stowe, Vt., a cosmopolitan ski resort community, estimates that 25 percent of the travel agency's business is to the Third World.

—*Fashion.* The Nehru jacket, now long gone, was only the beginning. Americans are making greater use of Asian-design rugs and Latin clothes. In 1986 Bloomingdale's department store launched a six-week promotion of Indian products and culture. Bloomingdale's chairman said the company had a firm commitment to maintain the continuity of Indian products in its stores. About the same time, the founders of the Banana Republic clothing store chain, former journalists, announced they would hike in Peru and Bolivia looking for new clothing ideas.

—*Sports.* Latins on major-league baseball teams are not a new phenomenon, though the numbers have grown. About 4 percent of all big-league baseball players came from Latin America in 1955. Today almost 11 percent do. Meanwhile, Third Worlders have started to play in other sports, particularly at the college level in track and basketball. Tiny Marist College, with players from five foreign countries, nearly upset sixth-ranked Georgia Tech in the 1986 NCAA basketball tournament. A New York City firm, the Harlem Third World Trade Institute, puts together college recruiting trips to Africa. Americans have imported a foreign sport, soccer, and youngsters lionized Brazilian star Pelé. And, like everything else, there is a reverse side, too. When George Scott's career was over in major-league baseball, he joined the Mexico City Tigers.

—*Food*. Perhaps no other pastime is more an expression of culture than what we eat—and more and more of what we eat comes from developing countries. C.F. Sauer IV, of the Richmond-based C.F. Sauer Co. in Virginia, says Third World influences have boosted interest in exotic spices the company sells. Getting those spices complicates his business: "The Sikh uprising in India last year [1984] had a profound effect on the distribution system for celery seed. For a while, it was very difficult to obtain and the price nearly doubled. Right now, they're getting too much rain in Indonesia and Brazil and the price of pepper is skyrocketing."[1] And it's not just food that is internationalized. So is what we drink. One of the newest foreign beers to arrive on our shores is Tusker. A Milwaukee company distributes the Kenyan brew, of course.

What's more, Americans watch Chinese-language movies on cable television, read Latin American novelists, tap their toes to reggae music, and keep llamas, native to the Andes, around the house as pets. In its Third World series, the Wooster, Ohio, *Daily Record* reported that orchids and other flowers at the local Flower and Bridal Show came from developing countries. And Third World influences have even brightened beauty contests in the Deep South, where girl-watching is something of an art form. The winner of the Miss Hattiesburg contest several years ago had a

---

1. The Associated Press story in *The Washington Post*, August 19, 1985.

Nicaraguan mother. Her act in the talent competition? The flamenco.

The story below expands on the theme of changing American eating habits.

# Local Eateries Are a Real Melting Pot

BLOOMINGTON, Ind.—At first glance, the Indiana Sweet Shop is a piece of Americana: the two plate-glass windows, the tiger-striped floor, the nine stools along the L-shaped counter, the portly old popcorn maker, the Coca-Cola menu on the wall.

But look again. The loyal lunchtime crowd that bellies up to the counter is eating fried rice and kimchi, a pungent spicy cabbage dish as Korean as cheeseburgers are American.

"We sell more eggrolls than egg sandwiches," says Sophia Kim, a gentle Korean woman who runs the shop with her three children.

The Indiana Sweet Shop is a vivid example of the way interdependence with developing countries transforms American culture and the way business caters to these new tastes.

A quarter of a century ago, eating out in this Midwestern town meant "steak, 'taters, and salad," says Kevin Brennan, president of the Bloomington Area Restaurant Association.

Today, Bloomington dines on Lebanese, Chinese, Korean, Ethiopian, Afghan, Yugoslav, and Mexican food. Altogether 20 to 25 percent of the formal restaurants in town serve other than American and Western European fare, Brennan figures.

Many of the longtime local restaurants have broadened their menus to include Mexican and other Third World foods.

Bloomington has a special link with the Third World. It is the home of Indiana University, which attracts students from all over the world.

140

Sophia Kim came in 1961 with her Korean husband, who studied for a year at IU and settled in the community. Nine years ago she bought the Indiana Sweet Shop, which has stood next to the Indiana Theatre, in the heart of town, since 1932.

But exotic eating habits are not confined to university towns. The number of Oriental restaurants in the United States increased by about 23 percent between 1983 and 1985, says Marilyn Goler of the Restaurant Consulting Group in Evanston, Ill.

After pizza, says Warren Spangler, executive vice president of the Indiana Restaurant Association Inc., "our growth [in the state] has been Mexican number one, Chinese number two."

Restaurants are ideal businesses for immigrants from developing nations. They require low initial capital and provide work for entire families, who often have sketchy command of English at first. Moreover, ethnic restaurants have, by definition, a niche in the market, says Morton J. Marcus, director of IU's Indiana Business Research Center.

"The same thing applied 50 years ago for Italian restaurants when you had large numbers of Italian immigrants," Marcus says.

Immigration from developing countries, however, only partly explains the increase in restaurants with Third World menus. The recent takeoff of such restaurants is primarily a consequence of strictly domestic cultural shifts, Marcus says.

With more single-person households, more women working, and more disposable income, people eat out more. No longer limited to the dishes they know how to cook, Americans can sample a wider variety of food.

Coupled with these changes is concern about health. "Nowadays people are scared about eating hamburgers, too much cholesterol," Mrs. Kim says. Food from developing countries makes liberal use of fresh vegetables and fish.

Kidan Hagos, an Ethiopian who opened her second restaurant in February, takes pride in serving no canned or frozen food. "People in my country don't have everything they want," she says, "but they eat healthier foods."

There's also the price. A lunch of eggrolls, fried rice, and sweet-and-sour chicken costs $2.98 at Mrs. Kim's.

Greater ease of travel has whetted American appetites for new foods, says Brennan, who is also a food manager at the university union. "As we have become more able to eat food in other lands," he says, "we have brought them back."

Capitalizing on these new eating habits, Bill Ben, a Korean-American, has started A-Ri-Rang, a fast-food Oriental restaurant in Bloomington. "The next McDonald's in the business will be the one that puts together a successful concept and operation for Oriental fast food," he says.

Ben, a smooth, corporate-savvy executive and the son of a Korean restaurateur in Omaha, Neb., started three Oriental fast-food restaurants in his hometown and launched an eggroll company that sells to delicatessens and restaurants. He recently joined forces with Wharfside Restaurants Inc., a multifranchise company based in Indiana.

The Bloomington A-Ri-Rang is their first joint effort. Ben is working to perfect the operation, which uses computerized cooking times and premeasured ingredients. The staff doesn't do anything more complicated than cut vegetables.

The system, he says, "doesn't require a single Oriental person on the premises."

Ben's next move is into Indianapolis. He says a study shows the city can support 12 of his fast-food restaurants.

Although Americans may have found it easier to try new foods because they eat out more, they are now experimenting at home. Robert Haft, president of Crown Books, a large retailer, says that his sales of Oriental cookbooks are up 50 percent since 1983.

Beaumont Hung, who operates the Lung Cheung, one of the more successful Chinese restaurants in town, has appeared on public television to teach cooking. He is thinking about doing a video on preparing Chinese food.

Majid Matus, a Libyan, opened the Sahara Mart three years ago. At first most customers were foreign students; today 15 to 20 percent of the people who pick from the shelves of canned curry cuttlefish and fresh tamarind are Americans. Matus quickly ran out of the 600 copies of the Middle Eastern recipe book he put together. People call him up regularly for cooking advice.

Bloomington has two other Middle Eastern and two Oriental food stores.

Two American chefs have gone to work for Ms. Hagos to learn to cook Ethiopian food. They make less money than in their previous jobs but want to widen their skills and, she says, grow with her business.

Ms. Hagos, who has plans to expand to Indianapolis, is determined to prepare only authentic food from Ethiopia and other developing countries. Other Third World restaurateurs have found it necessary to compromise.

Recognizing that people are concerned about salt intake, Mrs. Kim does not use monosodium glutamate in her food, she says. She tried twice to serve native ginseng tea to her customers. "Sometimes I just let them taste, but they didn't like it."

Hung stopped serving chicken the way the Chinese eat it, with the skin still on. He doesn't bother with shark's fin soup and abalone, Chinese favorites. His lunchtime buffet includes mashed potatoes.

"If I write pelave [on the menu], people don't eat," says Akram Azam, an Afghani who opened a meat market and restaurant in January. "If I write sirloin strip in onion sauce on rice and salad plate, people eat it."

Of course, cultural interchange is a two-way street. Says Hung, a native of Hong Kong, "There's nothing better than New York strip and baked potato."

—**John Maxwell Hamilton**
*The Christian Science Monitor*
April 14, 1986

# 17

# America: A Third World Classroom

IN KARACHI BOOKSTORES, Pakastani youngsters browse through *Barron's* guide to American colleges. In Amman, Jordan, terrorists bomb meeting rooms used by American college recruiters. In Malaysia, political leaders worry that their young people studying in the United States will consort with Islamic fundamentalists—and become political threats when they return home.

But the most visible signs of American collegiate ties to the Third World are right on U.S. campuses.

At the beginning of the 1985-86 academic year, a record 342,113 foreigners studied at some 2,500 American colleges. That continued a trend that began in the early 1970s, when rising petroleum prices gave oil-exporting countries of the Third World the capital to finance foreign schooling for their young people. Although oil prices have since fallen and worldwide economic malaise and levels of indebtedness have stymied growth for other developing countries, the number of Third World students attending American universities is still rising. Of the 10 countries that sent the most students to the United States in 1985, eight belonged to the developing world: Taiwan, Malaysia, Nigeria, Iran, South Korea, India, Venezuela, and Hong Kong. The heavy Asian representation reflects that region's relative strong economic performance in recent years.

Universities attach great importance to foreigners, who currently make up almost 3 percent of total enrollment. The number of American students pursuing college degrees has dropped off since 1983 and will likely decline further as a result of a projected 17.7 percent decline in American high school graduates during the decade ending in 1993. Importing foreign students is a way to keep classrooms filled.

The implications of foreign enrollments are certain to receive attention in coming years. Educators already worry about the numbers of foreigners reaching the level at Northrop University in California, where non-Americans account for more than 55 percent of the student body. The Massachusetts Institute of Technology limits foreign student enrollment to 29 percent in each graduate school department. Other schools worry about the effectiveness of foreign-born graduate students working as teaching assistants. The University of Pittsburgh refunded tuition payments to students who protested that they couldn't understand a Chinese instructor. Worried about foreign students graduating into American jobs, Congress has considered legislation that would require foreigners to return home for at least two years after completing their studies.

John F. Reichard, executive vice president of the National Association for Foreign Student Affairs, argues "We have a lot to gain by educating the people who will be the future leaders of countries around the world." The Reagan administration has been keen to combat the Soviet Union scholarship program, which raised the number of Central Americans studying in its universities by 3,000 percent between 1977 and 1982. Among other things, the administration pressed Congress to underwrite scholarships. The first beneficiaries from Central America arrived in the United States in early 1986 to attend colleges across the country, from Oregon to Vermont.

When WSAZ-TV in Huntington, W.Va., put together its "Connections: The Third World" series, one of the first places it looked was local Marshall University. Executive editor and anchor Bob Brunner centered the piece on the strong visual images presented by the Third World students themselves. The story appeared on March 1, 1986.

# Foreign Students A Huntington Resource

**Bob Brunner (News Center 3 studio):** This evening we continue our series of reports called "Connections: The Third World," looking at the impact of developing nations on our region—an impact we usually don't think much about. Tonight, Third World students.

**Brunner (on tape):** The campus of Marshall University, Huntington, W. Va. Nine thousand full-time students make an obvious economic impact on the surrounding community and more than a hundred of them are from developing nations—what we call the Third World. They spend an average of $12,000 a year each to study here, bringing more than a million dollars to the local economy. Most are studying mathematics, business, economics. Many will assume leadership roles in their countries when they return. So how do we view them? How do they view us? The perspectives are a bit different and worth a moment's consideration.

**Salah Elahjji, Libya:** Some kind of [misunderstanding] happens between the government here and back there. That's when [people] care, and they want to know everything. But, when they live their regular life, they don't really care.

**Basel Issa, Kuwait:** When my government plays the oil [market] and they need some more money to build a hospital, a lot of people in the Western world say, ''Oh, God, the Western world is . . . going to suffer now.'' But they can't understand that it's for our own good, and it's our own oil. We need to develop . . . using that oil.

**Farukh Hamed, Pakistan:** When I go home, I will take the education with me, the good ideas and the bad ideas that I have picked up about this country. And I'm going to give people in Pakistan a true image, basing it on my five years' stay that I've been here.

**Satha Sitheravellu, Malaysia:** Some people don't know much about Malaysia. They [ask] me . . . do Malaysians live on treetops? I'm sad for their ignorance.

**Alowell Akatobi, Nigeria:** I don't think America is a bad society. It is a good society, in a way. You know, it is a free society where you are allowed to [do] whatever you want to do. But at times there is a lot of, you know, discrimination, racism, you know.

**Brunner (on tape):** And the head of the International Students Program wishes more of us would begin to realize the potential benefit of more interaction with these young people.

**Judith Assad, International Students Coordinator:** I am often disappointed that the campus doesn't take more note of the students. And I think a lot of it has to do with the business climate here, that students are more concerned about getting a degree and getting a job than they are about turning aside to learn anything about anything other than where they're from themselves.

**Brunner (on tape):** So yes, Third World students are a million-dollar economic resource for the Huntington tri-state area. But, even more important, and often ignored, they are a great human resource.

**Brunner (studio):** And all told there are more than 700 Third World students at other West Virginia colleges and universities, another 300 in eastern Kentucky, and more than 500 in southern Ohio.

# 18 ———————————————————————

# Drawing Opinions
# From the Facts

THE STORIES in this book raise issues that Americans must address. As such, they are grist for analytical and opinion articles. Below are two pieces that fall into those categories.

The first is an excerpt from an article by Loren Ghiglione, editor of the *Bristol* (Conn.) *Press.* In the fall of 1985, the paper decided to run a special section to coincide with a local referendum on the Supreme Court decision establishing the right to an abortion. Seeing this as an opportunity to include an international angle, Ghiglione wrote a story analyzing in detail the Reagan administration's decision not to provide funds for Third World family planning programs that support abortion. From a strong factual base he led readers to the conclusions, excerpted below, about how these policies may affect their lives.

Richard Mial wrote the second piece, an editorial, when his newspaper, the *La Crosse Tribune*, kicked off a seven-day series on the Wisconsin community's local Third World ties. However wide the range of opinion on interdependence may be, few would disagree with his main point: "... as a nation and as a community, we can run but we can't hide from the impact of world events on our daily lives."

# Size of World Family
# A Bristol Issue

BRISTOL, Conn.—The White House anti-abortion policy may not reflect Americans' views or be in their interest. A 1984 Gallup survey asked whether Americans thought the United States should provide family planning support in countries where abortion is legal; 72 percent said yes.

Dr. Sheldon Segal, director of population sciences at the Rockefeller Foundation, summarizes the Gallup results: "Americans. . . overwhelmingly reject the notion that the United States should tie family planning assistance to others' policies on abortion; they believe that family planning assistance to poor countries should be increased or remain the same; and they are convinced that rapid population growth hurts economic development in poor countries."

What's bad for the economy of developing countries could be bad for the United States. The population/food crunch fuels social unrest that can lead to coups and other forms of civil unrest. "Political disorder," writes Carol Lancaster, director of the African studies program at Georgetown University's School of Foreign Service, "can provide opportunities for an expansion in the influence of the Soviet Union and its allies; the dangers of superpower confrontation may increase."

Also, it's difficult for the United States and other industrial countries to trade with starving, debt-ridden nations. Secretary of State George Shultz said in mid-1984, "Our exports to Africa have dropped by 50 percent in the last three years." And Africa's petroleum and mineral resources—vital cobalt, manganese, chromium, and platinum—threaten to become less accessible.

Finally, rapid population growth stimulates poor countries' need for increased economic development aid, more expensive to the United States and other donor countries than the family planning assistance that may better alleviate the population problem in the first place.

If only in U.S. self-interest, American family planning assistance abroad should continue, say population experts. And that assistance, argue critics of current U.S. foreign aid policy, needs to be judged on its merits, not held hostage by the administration's anti-abortion ideology.

—**Loren Ghiglione**
*Bristol Press*
October 30, 1985

# *Interdependence A Reality in La Crosse*

LA CROSSE, Wis.—The notion of a shrinking world has become a cliché. It remains true nonetheless. As the *La Crosse Tribune* today begins a series of stories on our area's ties and connections to the developing world, let us share with you a story.

A couple in La Crosse adopted a young Korean boy a few years ago. He's doing fine, has learned English, and is performing well in school. But plenty of adjustments had to be made, not the least of which was overcoming the language barrier.

On the first day of school, in a city school which has a program to teach English to non-native speakers, the boy became happy and excited when he noticed two other Asian children. And they were excited, too. As they eagerly joined together to finally communicate with other children in their native tongues, they found they could not. One was a Korean, another Hmong, and the third Cambodian.

If you need any reminder of a wider world, you need look no further than La Crosse's Asian refugee community, some 1,500 strong. These are for the most part Hmong people from the mountains of Laos, who were recruited by the CIA to fight on the side of Americans against the North Vietnamese. After the fall of

151

Saigon in 1975, the Hmong were persecuted and murdered. Survivors found their way here. Today an estimated 800,000 Indochinese refugees live in the United States.

But that is not the whole story of the ties between Main Street America and the Third World. If you wonder what relationship events in the developing world have to our lives, consider:

—Trane Co. in La Crosse has for years sold its products in the Middle East and Asia.

—A new company, Albraze International, formerly the brazed aluminum division of Trane, is targeting Third World nations as customers. Under Trane Co., that division sold brazed aluminum heat exchangers to Indonesia and Algeria.

—Indus Industries, another spin-off of a larger firm (it used to be the microfiche division of NCR Corp.), plans sales to China and other Far Eastern nations.

—Down used in coats and comforters produced by Gillette Industries Inc., of La Crosse, comes from China.

—Much of the competition for La Crosse Footwear Inc., formerly the La Crosse Rubber Mills, is from Third World nations.

—And even the G. Heileman Brewing Co., an economic bulwark in our community, may see competition from Third World beers—only the latest event in a long-running marketing battle involving imports.

Not all ties are business related.

—When the president of Botswana looked for an American college for his daughter, he chose Luther College in tiny Decorah, Iowa.

—Foreign students, many from Third World nations, make up a small but significant minority at La Crosse's institutions of higher education. In fact, the outgoing student body president at the University of Wisconsin-La Crosse, Stanley Mugeki, is from Kenya.

—The 700-member La Crosse-based Franciscan Sisters of Perpetual Adoration has a long history of involvement in Third World nations, particularly in Latin America. And other local church groups have also had international projects, including a La Crosse group of Assemblies of God lay people who built much-needed schools in Ecuador and Haiti over the last three years.

Those are just a few of the highlights of the *Tribune*'s series, which will run throughout the week. But what do these events and developments mean? We're not here to argue that a smaller, more interdependent world is good or bad; that is a reality that we cannot change.

What we do argue is that daily events in the world, coupled with American policy decisions, do matter in your life, in ways more direct than you might realize.

The relative strength of the dollar as opposed to other world currencies and the impact of government trade policies and sanctions imposed against the Soviet Union for invading Afghanistan all have an effect here at home, on Main Street America.

You may choose to ignore those implications. But our message is that, as a nation and as a community, we can run but we can't hide from the impact of world events on our daily lives.

—**Richard Mial**
*La Crosse Tribune*
April 20, 1986

# Appendix 1

# The Sources

## Chapter One
### Manufacturing Trade: The Two-Way Street

Chase Econometrics Inc.
150 Monument Road
Bala Cynwyd, Pa. 19004
(215) 667-6000

The Conference Board
845 Third Avenue
New York, N.Y. 10022
(212) 759-0900

International Trade Administration
U.S. Department of Commerce
14th Street and Constitution Ave.,
   N.W.
Washington, D.C. 20230
(202) 377-3808
(The Commerce Department's U.S.
Foreign & Commercial Service has
offices in 70 cities.)

International Trade Commission
701 E Street, N.W.
Washington, D.C. 20436
(202) 523-0235
(The ITC has reports on specific
industries.)

National Association of
   Manufacturers
1776 F Street, N.W.
Washington, D.C. 20006
(202) 637-3000

U.S. Chamber of Commerce
International Division
1615 H Street, N.W.
Washington, D.C. 20062
(202) 463-5460

U.S. Council for International
   Business
1155 15th Street, N.W.
Suite 811
Washington, D.C. 20005
(202) 466-2453

Wharton Econometric Forecasting
   Associates
3624 Science Center
Philadelphia, Pa. 19104
(215) 386-9000

## Chapter Two
### Third World Imports: Good Business

(See "Manufacturing Trade: The
Two-Way Street" above.)

## Chapter Three
### Third World Imports Keep U.S. Industries Humming

Bureau of Mines
U.S. Department of the Interior
2401 E Street, N.W.
Washington, D.C. 20241
(202) 634-1004

International Economic Policy
  Association
1400 I Street, N.W.
Suite 510
Washington, D.C. 20005
(202) 898-2020

Trade Information and Cost
  Reports Staff
Foreign Trade Division
U.S. Department of
Commerce/Bureau of Census
Suitland, Md. 20233
(301) 763-5140
(The staff annually publishes a
complete list of imports entitled
*U.S. Imports for Consumption and
General Imports.*)

**Chapter Four**
**Learning To Live With Third
World Markets**

(See "Manufacturing Trade: The
Two-Way Street" above.)

**Chapter Five**
**America's New Farmers' Market**

American Soybean Association
777 Craig Road
St. Louis, Mo. 63141-7164
(314) 432-1600

Foreign Agricultural Service
U.S. Department of Agriculture
14th Street and Independence
Avenue, S.W.
Washington, D.C. 20250
(202) 447-7115

National Association of Wheat
  Growers
415 Second Street, N.E.
Suite 300
Washington, D.C. 20002
(202) 547-7800

U.S. Wheat Associates
1620 I Street, N.W.
Suite 801
Washington, D.C. 20006
(202) 463-0999

**Chapter Six**
**Hometown Diplomats**

National Association of State
  Development Agencies
444 North Capitol Street, N.W.
Suite 526
Washington, D.C. 20001
(202) 624-5411

National Governors' Association
444 North Capitol Street, N.W.
Suite 250
Washington, D.C. 20001
(202) 624-5300

Sister Cities International
1625 I Street, N.W.
Suite 424
Washington, D.C. 20006
(202) 293-5504

**Chapter Seven**
**Banking on Development**

American Bankers Association
1120 Connecticut Avenue, N.W.
Washington, D.C. 20036
(202) 467-4000

External Debt Division
The World Bank
1818 H Street, N.W.
Washington, D.C. 20433
(202) 473-3868

Export-Import Bank of the United
  States
811 Vermont Avenue, N.W.
Washington, D.C. 20571
(202) 566-2117

Federal Deposit Insurance
 Corporation
550 17th Street, N.W.
Washington, D.C. 20429
(202) 898-6996

Federal Financial Institutions
 Examination Council
1776 G Street, N.W.
Suite 701
Washington, D.C. 20006
(202) 357-0177
(800) 424-4334

Institute for International
 Economics
11 Dupont Circle, N.W.
Suite 620
Washington, D.C. 20036
(202) 328-0583

Institute of International Finance
2000 Pennsylvania Ave., N.W.
Suite 8500
Washington, D.C. 20006
(202) 857-3600

## Chapter Eight
## Third World Investment: Here and There

International Finance Corporation
1818 H Street, N.W.
Washington, D.C. 20433
(202) 676-9331
(The IFC is an arm of the World
Bank responsible for promoting
private investment in developing
countries.)

National Resource Economics
 Division
Economic Research Service
U.S. Department of Agriculture
1301 New York Avenue, N.W.
Washington, D.C. 20005-4788
(202) 786-1425
(This division of the ERS keeps
records of all land purchase by
foreigners in the United States.)

Office of Trade and Investment
 Analysis
International Trade Administration
U.S. Department of Commerce
14th Street and Pennsylvania
 Avenue, N.W.
Washington, D.C. 20230
(202) 377-3118
(This office follows manufacturing
investment in the United States and
abroad.)

Overseas Private Investment
 Corporation
1615 M Street, N.W.
Washington, D.C. 20527
(202) 457-7093
(800) 457-7010
(OPIC, a U.S. government agency,
promotes private investment in
developing countries.)

## Chapter Nine
## Foreign Aid: Helping Americans

International Food Policy Research
Institute
1776 Massachusetts Avenue, N.W.
Washington, D.C. 20036-1998
(202) 862-5600

Overseas Development Council
1717 Massachusetts Avenue, N.W.
Suite 501
Washington, D.C. 20036
(202) 234-8701

Society for International
 Development
Washington Chapter
1401 New York Avenue, N.W.
Suite 1100
Washington, D.C. 20005
(202) 347-1800

United Nations Development
 Programme
One United Nations Plaza
New York, N.Y. 10017
(212) 906-5309

U.S. Agency for International
Development
320 21st Street, N.W.
Washington, D.C. 20523
(202) 663-1451

The World Bank
1818 H Street, N.W.
Washington, D.C. 20433
(202) 477-5606

**Chapter Ten**
**Homegrown Foreign Aid**

CARE
660 First Avenue
New York, N.Y. 10016
(212) 686-3110

Catholic Relief Services
1011 First Avenue
New York, N.Y. 10022
(212) 838-4700

Church World Service
475 Riverside Drive
New York, N.Y. 10115
(212) 870-2079

InterAction (American Council for
Voluntary International Action)
200 Park Avenue South
New York, N.Y. 10003
(212) 777-8210

Peace Corps
806 Connecticut Avenue, N.W.
Washington, D.C. 20526
(202) 254-5010

Peace Corps Institute
c/o William Josephson
Fried, Frank, Harris, Shriver &
Jacobson
One New York Plaza
New York, N.Y. 10004
(212) 820-8220
(The institute has lists, by city of
residence, of former Peace Corps
volunteers.)

The Population Council
One Dag Hammarskjold Plaza
New York, N.Y. 10017
(212) 644-1300

Save the Children
Wilten Road
Westport, Conn. 06880
(800) 243-5075

United States Committee for
UNICEF
331 East 38th Street
New York, N.Y. 10016
(212) 686-5522

**Chapter Eleven**
**"Hello, This Is Montego Bay":**
**The Information Revolution**

Berkeley Roundtable on the
International Economy
215 Moses Hall
University of California
Berkeley, Calif. 94720
(415) 642-3067
(BRIE specializes in policy-oriented
studies on the interaction between
high-technology developments and
the international economy.)

Data Entry Management
Association
750 Summer Street
Stamford, Conn. 06901
(203) 967-3500

Office of Service Industries
U.S. Department of Commerce
14th Street and Constitution
Avenue, N.W.
Washington, D.C. 20230
(202) 377-3575

Office of Technology Assessment
U.S. Congress
Washington, D.C. 20510
(202) 224-9241

Service Employees International
Union
1313 L Street, N.W.
Washington, D.C. 20005
(202) 898-3200

## Chapter Twelve _____
**Third World Ecology: A First World Concern**

Agriculture Research Service
National Program Leader for
Germplasm
Beltsville Agriculture Research
Center, West
Beltsville, Md. 20705
(301) 344-3311

Environmental Policy Institute
218 D Street, S.E.
Washington, D.C. 20003
(202) 544-2600

Global Tomorrow Coalition
1325 G Street, N.W.
Suite 1003
Washington, D.C. 20005
(202) 879-3040

National Audubon Society
645 Pennsylvania Avenue, S.E.
Washington, D.C. 20003
(202) 547-9009

National Wildlife Federation
1412 16th Street, N.W.
Washington, D.C. 20036
(202) 637-3773

Natural Resources Defense Council
Inc.
122 East 42nd Street
New York, N.Y. 10168
(212) 949-0049

World Resources Institute
1735 New York Avenue, N.W.
Suite 400
Washington, D.C. 20006
(202) 638-6300

World Wildlife Fund
1255 23rd Street, N.W.
Suite 200
Washington, D.C. 20037
(202) 293-4800

## Chapter Thirteen _____
**When the Third World Sneezes...**

Animal and Plant Health Inspection
Service
U.S. Department of Agriculture
Federal Building
6505 Belcrest Road
Hyattsville, Md. 20782
(301) 436-7799
(APHIS has regional offices.)

Center for Disease Control
1600 Clifton Road, N.E.
Atlanta, Ga. 30333
(404) 329-3311

Pan American Health Organization
525 23rd Street, N.W.
Washington, D.C. 20037
(202) 861-3459

## Chapter Fourteen _____
**Global Drug Addiction**

Bureau of International Narcotics
Matters
U.S. Department of State
2201 C Street, N.W.
Washington, D.C. 20520
(202) 647-8464
(Country desk officers can also
give details on specific countries.)

Drug Enforcement Administration
1405 I Street, N.W.
Washington, D.C. 20537
(202) 633-1469
(DEA has at least one office in
every state.)

Select Committee on Narcotics
  Abuse & Control
U.S. House of Representatives
Washington, D.C. 20515
(202) 226-3040
(Other congressional committees are
also concerned with drug issues.)

## Chapter Fifteen
## Immigrants: Why They Come, What They Bring

Bureau of Census
U.S. Department of Commerce
Suitland, Md. 20233
(301) 763-4040

Bureau of Refugee Programs
U.S. Department of State
2201 G Street, N.W.
Washington, D.C. 20520
(202) 663-1033

Division of Foreign Labor
  Certifications
Employment and Training
  Administration
U.S. Department of Labor
200 Constitution Avenue, N.W.
Washington, D.C. 20210
(202) 724-3770

Educational Commission for
  Foreign Medical Graduates
3624 Market Street
Philadelphia, Pa. 19104
(215) 386-5900

Immigration and Naturalization
  Service
10th Street and Constitution
Avenue, N.W.
Washington, D.C. 20530
(202) 633-2007

National Research Council
2101 Constitution Avenue, N.W.
Washington, D.C. 20418
(202) 334-2138

Office of Refugee Resettlement
U.S. Department of Health and
  Human Services
330 C Street, S.W.
Washington, D.C. 20201
(202) 245-0418

U.S. Committee for Refugees
815 15th Street, N.W.
Suite 610
Washington, D.C. 20005
(202) 667-0782

## Chapter Sixteen
## A Taste of Third World Culture

*Food*

International Life Sciences Institute
Nutrition Foundation Inc.
1126 16th Street, N.W.
Suite 111
Washington, D.C. 20036
(202) 872-0778

National Restaurant Association
311 First Street, N.W.
Washington, D.C. 20001
(202) 638-6100

Restaurant Consulting Group
1599 Maple Avenue
Evanston, Ill. 60201
(312) 869-8600

*Travel*

American Society of Travel Agents
4400 MacArthur Boulevard, N.W.
Washington, D.C. 20007
(202) 965-7520

Subcommittee on Business, Trade
  & Tourism
U. S. Senate
Washington, D.C. 20510
(202) 224-4852

Subcommittee on Commerce,
Transportation & Tourism
U.S. House of Representatives
Washington, D.C. 20515
(202) 226-3160

U.S. Travel and Tourism
Administration
U.S. Department of Commerce
14th Street and Constitution
Avenue, N.W.
Washington, D.C. 20230
(202) 377-0137

**Chapter Seventeen**
**America: A Third World**
**Classroom**

Council for International Exchange
of Scholars
11 Dupont Circle, N.W.
Suite 300
Washington, D.C. 20036-1257
(202) 939-5400

Experiment in International
Living/School for International
Training
Kipling Road
Brattleboro, Vt. 05301
(802) 257-7751
(This organization is engaged in
international student exchange,
academic and training programs in
international affairs, management
and language training for teachers,
and development and refugee
assistance projects overseas.)

Institute of International Education
809 United Nations Plaza
New York, N.Y. 10017
(212) 883-8200

National Association for Foreign
Student Affairs
1860 19th Street, N.W.
Washington, D.C. 20009
(202) 462-4811

United States Information Agency
Bureau of Educational and Cultural
Affairs
301 Fourth Street, S.W.
Washington, D.C. 20547
(202) 485-2949

**Chapter Eighteen**
**Drawing Opinions From Facts**

(See all of the above.)

# Appendix 2 ————————————————————

# Readers Care

## By John Mauro
### Director, Media General Research

ONE OF THE MAJOR IMPEDIMENTS to improving coverage of international events is the traditional journalistic belief, mentioned in the introduction to this book, that readers don't care, that they won't read stories about Europe, let alone Third World nations. *New York Times* columnist James Reston summed it up in a statement that could be applied to any region of the developing world. ''Americans will do anything for Latin America except read about it.''

However persuasive this point of view has been, it is wrong. Americans will read news about the Third World, especially when it is presented in ways that seem relevant to their lives.

The basis for these assertions comes from two polls carried out in connection with stories appearing in this volume. The first poll examined readership of ''Main Street Mississippi & The Third World,'' the series appearing in The *Hattiesburg American* over a five-day period in November 1984. Dr. Susan Siltanen of the School of Communication at the University of Southern Mississippi directed the survey. The second poll, under my direction, looked at readership attitudes toward two stories appearing in the *Richmond Times-Dispatch,* entitled ''The Third World Comes Home.'' The stories ran together on November 24, 1985, and are reprinted in chapter one.

Both polls showed strong readership. With regard to the Hattiesburg series, an average of 48.5 percent of those polled—which included respondents who hadn't read any stories in the paper—could, at the least, recall each of the six main articles. The Richmond poll found that 60 percent of those who had read the newspaper remembered seeing at least one of the two stories, which ran under a common headline; 50 percent reported reading either one or both of the stories.

Equally significant was the overwhelming interest in having more Third World stories. Both polls were conducted in two phases, one before the series appeared and one afterward. More than seven out of 10 respondents in both post-polls thought that newspapers should provide more news about developing countries.

These polls are not the first to demonstrate that readers have greater interest in foreign affairs than editors and reporters generally think they have. A Harris poll in the late 1970s found that 41 percent of the public expressed a strong interest in international news, but only 5 percent of editors and reporters, who were also surveyed, believed that the public had a strong interest.[1] Other polls have shown that Americans will, indeed, read foreign news. A study by the Newspaper Advertising Bureau conducted during the Argentine-British conflict over the Falkland Islands found that front page readership of international stories averaged 54 percent.[2]

What makes the Hattiesburg and Richmond polls especially interesting is that they (a) looked at softer feature-type stories, not at hard-breaking news such as the Falkland crisis, and (b) involved strictly Third World countries, in which Americans are supposed to have the least interest.

As noted just above, both polls were conducted in two parts, with questions asked before and after the stories ran. This permitted the polls to look at attitude changes, which resulted in several other significant findings:

—Most people believe that, in the abstract, the world is interdependent. In both the "before" and "after" polls in Hattiesburg,

---

1. "Record," *The Quill*, April 1978, p. 7.

2. "Meeting Readers' Multiple Needs: Content and Readership of News and Features in the Daily Press," Newspaper Research Project, Newspaper Advertising Bureau Inc., March 1984. For other discussions of reader and viewer interest in international news, see Lee Bogart, "The Public's Use and Perception of Newspapers," *Public Opinion Quarterly* (Winter 1984), and Haluk Sahin, Dennis K. Davis, and John P. Robinson, "Television as a Source of International News: What Gets Across and What Doesn't," in *Television Coverage of International News,* ed. William Adams (Norwood, N.J.: Abley, 1983), pp. 229-244.

more than 85 percent either "strongly agreed" or "agreed" that the world is interdependent and that "what happens in one country influences other countries." But in the first survey, respondents did not believe this interdependence had much to do with their personal lives. Less than one-half in the pretest either "strongly agreed" or "agreed" that political and social upheavals in the Third World have an impact on Hattiesburg or that Third World economic growth promotes economic growth in Hattiesburg. The Richmond poll, discussed in more detail at the end of this appendix, had a similar outcome.

—Third World stories, such as those that appeared in the Hattiesburg and Richmond newspapers, sharpen awareness that interdependence has an impact on everyone's life. The percentage of respondents who agreed that economic growth in poorer countries promotes economic growth in Hattiesburg increased by almost one-third (from 42 percent to 55 percent); the percentage of people who agreed that political upheavals in developing countries make a difference at home increased by almost one-sixth (from 41 percent to 48 percent). The Richmond poll showed that the improvement levels in *understanding* the need to know about events in developing countries and in *awareness* that interdependence involved them personally were more than twice as high for readers of the stories than for non-readers.

*Replication*

Others can easily duplicate the polls done in Hattiesburg and Richmond. Details on the Richmond survey and a sample questionnaire that follows this appendix may be of help to those who wish to do so.[3]

In general, the surveys are typical pre- and posttest designs. The condition is assessed, a stimulus is implemented, and the condition is reassessed. In this case, we first measured the levels of understanding and awareness about Third World countries. The newspaper ran the stories. We made another measurement. Readers

---

3. For more details on the Hattiesburg poll, see "Hometown Newspaper Coverage of Developing Countries: Its Effect on Perceived Interdependence of Nations" (Paper presented at the Southern Speech Communications Convention, Winston-Salem, N.C., April 11-13, 1985). The Principal author is Susan A. Siltanen.

of the stories in Richmond were compared with non-readers, often called the control group.

Besides these measures, the survey asks other questions to determine demographic characteristics, news preferences, and news norms of the sample.

Polling can be done by telephone or by an in-home, face-to-face interview. Interviews in the home are obviously more expensive. Telephone interviews must include non-listed telephone numbers. This is usually accomplished by modified random digit dialing. Shopping center or street intercept interviews are not recommended. It is not essential that the same respondents be reinterviewed in the post-survey. Instead, a new sample may be drawn, but it must adhere to sound sampling theory, which stipulates that all elements in the universe have an equal chance of being selected.

*The Richmond Survey Method*

The Richmond survey was conducted through telephone interviews of a randomly selected sample of 551 men and women in listed and non-listed telephone homes in the Richmond urbanized area (city of Richmond and the counties of Henrico and Chesterfield). The sample represents 437,000 adults 18 years and older residing in telephone households in the survey area. Interviewing for this pretest was accomplished during November 8-18, 1985.

The pretest questionnaire included questions that established news norms and preferences using a paired comparison method, questions on awareness and understanding that would be used again in the posttest, and questions to describe the sample according to demographic characteristics.

The posttest was conducted on the evening of November 24, 1985, when the stories ran, and on the following day and evening until 10 p.m. among the *same persons* interviewed in the pretest. This was done to eliminate any bias that may result from sample variance.

Of the 551 adults sampled, 456, or 83 percent, were reached for the second interview. Men were reached significantly less than women and, although a straight tabulation of total adults showed that imbalance to make little difference, it was decided to weight the men to bring them into balance with women.

The posttest questionnaire included the five questions on awareness and understanding that were in the pretest questionnaire. In addition, it contained questions on readership of the test articles.

Sunday, November 24, 1985, when the articles ran, happened to be a bright, unseasonably warm day, which might have postponed some persons' reading of the Sunday newspaper. Normally, over 85 percent of the adults in the study area read the Sunday *Times-Dispatch*. On November 24, only 51 percent did.

*Summary of Findings*

Of all adults surveyed, 51 percent—which would translate into 223,000 adult readers in Virginia—said they had read that issue of the Sunday *Times-Dispatch* during the 30-hour interviewing period from 6 p.m. Sunday evening to 10 p.m. Monday night.

Of the 223,000 readers, 42 percent noticed the first story, which was on the tobacco industry; 33 percent, or 74,000 adults, read the story in part or whole.

The second story, on the shoe industry, achieved somewhat higher readership, probably because it dealt specifically with a neighboring community. Of the Sunday *Times-Dispatch* readers 51 percent noticed the shoe story, and 41 percent, or 91,000 adults, read all or part of the article.

The net notice of both stories came to 60 percent of the issue's readers and achieved a net readership of 50 percent, or 112,000 readers.

Positioning the stories together might be the reason why both received close readership scores. Of course, had the stories been located separately, the variance in readership might have caused other distortions.

Additionally, if the interviewing could have been done in-home, during which time copies of the front page of the newspaper could have been shown to the respondent, recall levels might have been higher.

The following tables illustrate the readership data.

## Percentage of Readers of Tobacco Industry Story

|  | All Adults | Adults Who Read Issue of Newspaper |
|---|---|---|
| Base: Total Sample | 100% (456) |  |
| Did Not Read Study Issue of Newspaper | 49 |  |
| Read Study Issue of Newspaper | 51 | 100 (231) |
| Noticed tobacco story | 21 | 42 |
| Read some or all of text | 17 | 33 |
| Less than one-half text | 6 | 11 |
| More than one-half text | 6 | 13 |
| All or almost all of text | 5 | 9 |
| Noticed, but did not read any text | 4 | 9 |

## Percentage of Readers of Shoe Story

|  | All Adults | Adults Who Read Issue of Newspaper |
|---|---|---|
| Base: Total Sample | 100% (456) |  |
| Did Not Read Study Issue of Newspaper | 49 |  |
| Read Study Issue of Newspaper | 51 | 100 (231) |
| Noticed shoe story | 26 | 51 |
| Read some or all of text | 21 | 41 |
| Less than one-half text | 6 | 11 |
| More than one-half text | 9 | 17 |
| All or almost all of text | 6 | 13 |
| Noticed, but did not read any text | 5 | 10 |

| Percentage of Readers of Either or Both Stories | | |
|---|---|---|
| | All Adults | Adults Who Read Issue of Newspaper |
| Base: Total Sample | 100% (456) | |
| Did Not Read Study Issue of Newspaper | 49 | |
| Read Study Issue of Newspaper | 51 | 100 (231) |
| Noticed either or both stories | 30 | 60 |
| Read either or both stories | 25 | 50 |
| Read tobacco story only | 4 | 9 |
| Read shoe story only | 9 | 17 |
| Read both stories | 12 | 24 |

Considering the unseasonably good weather, the manner in which the stories were presented, and the international scope of both stories, readership of 33 percent and 41 percent is as good as can be expected in this market for feature stories on international news. It compares favorably with the Hattiesburg results and with other studies as well.

The next question is what effect, if any, these stories had in changing the respondents' awareness and understanding of the need to know more about Third World countries.

Using the five questions in the Hattiesburg test, this study gauged responses before and after the stories appeared. At most, only two weeks had elapsed between the pre- and the posttest.

The five questions were the following:

*For awareness—*

"Do you agree or disagree that economic growth and progress in these poorer countries affect economics in Virginia?"

"Do you agree or disagree that political and social upheavals in these poorer countries affect Virginians?"

"Recently, there has been a great deal of talk about the interdependence of countries and that what happens in

one country influences other countries. Do you agree
or disagree that what happens in one country influences
another country?''

*For understanding—*

''Do you think it is important or not important to understand what is going on in poorer countries?''

''Do you think it is important or not important that
newspapers provide more news about what is going on
in poorer countries?''

A large majority of respondents agreed in the pretest that what
happens in Third World countries affects other countries.
Substantially fewer believe that what happens politically, socially,
and economically in the Third World actually affects Virginians'
lives.

A near unanimity existed in the pretest on the importance of
understanding what is going on in poorer countries and a
significantly strong majority extolled the importance of newspapers
providing more news about Third World countries. Perhaps the
high proportion of people who said Third World news is important
reflects responses to questions 14 and 15 in the pretest. In that
test, 76 percent of respondents said they read news about the Third
World. Of these, 78 percent said they read these stories
thoroughly.

Between the pre- and posttest a statistically significant
improvement occurred in the public's awareness that
interdependence actually has an impact on their lives. The increase
in awareness that what happens in one country affects another
did not increase as much, not surprising since it started from such
a high level.

| | | | Percentage Points |
|---|---|---|---|
| Awareness Variables: Percentage of All Adults Who Agreed | | | |
| | Pretest | Posttest | Improvement |
| Base: Total Sample | 100% (456) | 100% (456) | |
| Economic growth affects economics in Virginia | 55 | 67 | 12 |
| Political and social upheavals affect Virginians | 61 | 73 | 12 |
| Happenings in one country affect other countries | 81 | 85 | 4 |

The percentage of respondents thinking it important that they understand what is going on in the Third World and that newspapers need to provide more Third World news also improved, although not significantly. Again, when positive responses reach such high proportions, how much higher can they get?

| | | | Percentage Points |
|---|---|---|---|
| Understanding Variables: Percentage of All Adults Who Said "Important" | | | |
| | Pretest | Posttest | Improvement |
| Base: Total Sample | 100% (456) | 100% (456) | |
| Understand what is going on in poorer countries | 91 | 94 | 3 |
| Newspapers provide more news | 71 | 77 | 6 |

The question remains, however: Did awareness and understanding improve more among those who read the stories than among those who did not?

Although it seemed that the percentages for some categories were not likely to get any higher, they did, particularly among those who read either story or both.

For every variable listed on the following two tables, improvement of awareness and understanding was substantially greater among readers of the stories than among non-readers.

**Awareness Variables:**
**Percentage of Those Who Agreed: Non-Readers vs. Readers**

| | | Read Neither Story | Read One or Both Stories |
|---|---|---|---|
| Base: Respondents who agreed | | 100% (341) | 100% (115) |
| Economic growth affects economics in Virginia | Pretest | 54 | 59 |
| | Posttest | 64 | 75 |
| Percentage points improvement | | 10 | 16 |
| Political and social upheavals affect Virginians | Pretest | 58 | 68 |
| | Posttest | 69 | 83 |
| Percentage points improvement | | 11 | 15 |
| Happenings in one country affect other countries | Pretest | 79 | 86 |
| | Posttest | 83 | 92 |
| Percentage points improvement | | 4 | 6 |

**Understanding Variables:**
**Percentage of Those Who Said "Important": Non-Readers vs. Readers**

| | | Read Neither Story | Read One or Both Stories |
|---|---|---|---|
| Base: Respondents who said "Important" | | 100% (341) | 100% (115) |
| Understand what is going on in poorer countries | Pretest | 91 | 89 |
| | Posttest | 93 | 97 |
| Percentage points improvement | | 2 | 8 |
| Newspapers provide more news | Pretest | 72 | 68 |
| | Posttest | 76 | 81 |
| Percentage points improvement | | 4 | 13 |

A statistical method compares each respondent's answer before and after a stimulus is applied. In this case the stimulus is reading the stories. The method subtracts the response before from the response after, averages the differences for all respondents, and calculates the statistical significance.

Response in this study was coded so that this method of comparison could be applied.

The results show average improvement was greater among readers of the stories than among non-readers. The largest difference occurred in the belief that it is important for newspapers to provide more news about Third World countries.

Overall, in all five variables as a composite, the improvement level of awareness and understanding was 122 percent—more than twice as great among readers as among non-readers.*

| Improvement Levels: Averages of Awareness and Understanding | | |
|---|---|---|
| | Percentage of Improvement: Readers Over Non-Readers | |
| Economic growth affects economics in Virginia | + | 94 |
| Political and social upheavals affect Virginians | + | 50 |
| Happenings in one country affect other countries | + | 15 |
| Awareness Composite | + | 60 |
| Understand what is going on in poorer countries | + | 520 |
| Newspapers provide more news | + | 1,158 |
| Understanding Composite | + | 810 |
| Awareness and Understanding Composite | + | 122 |

---

* For more details on Richmond study, see "Hometown Newspaper Coverage of Developing Countries: Its Effect on Perceived Interdependence of Nations," Media General Reseach, December, 1985.

---

Card # 1-2                                    Telephone #

---

Case # 3-6                    Telephone Questionnaire

### ANALYSIS OF NEWSPAPER REPORTING
### ON DEVELOPING COUNTRIES
(Pretest)

Date_____ Time _____

Hello. This is 7-8_____ of _____.
We're doing a survey on attitudes and opinions concerning types of news stories
that appear in local newspapers and would appreciate a few minutes of your
time. We are not trying to sell you anything. Your telephone number was chosen
at random, and your answers will be combined with those of hundreds of others
in the Richmond area.

Are you 18 years or older?

( ) Yes
( ) No     *(DISCONTINUE INTERVIEW)*

First, I'd like to read some statements about news and newspapers that some
people agree with and others disagree with. Please tell me whether you agree
or disagree with these statements:

|  | Agree | Disagree | DK |
|---|---|---|---|
| 1. It is important to be informed about news and current events. | 9-3( ) | 1( ) | 2( ) |
| 2. So many other people follow the news and keep informed about it that it doesn't matter much whether I do. | 10-1( ) | 3( ) | 2( ) |
| 3. A good deal of news about current events isn't important enough to keep informed about. | 11-1( ) | 3( ) | 2( ) |
| 4. We all have a duty to keep ourselves informed about news and current events. | 12-3( ) | 1( ) | 2( ) |

**172**

These next questions are about Sunday newspaper readership. We're interested in whether you have read or looked into any part of the Sunday paper.

5. Have you ever read a Sunday newspaper?

   13-1( )Yes
     2( ) No  *(DISCONTINUE INTERVIEW)*

6. Which of the following Sunday newspapers, if any, did you happen to read or look into during the past four weeks?

   14-1( )Sunday *Petersburg Progress Index*
   15-2( )Sunday *Richmond Times-Dispatch*
   16-3( )Other Sunday paper(s)_____
                                    *(WRITE IN)*
   17-4( )Read no Sunday paper in past four weeks  *(DISCONTINUE INTERVIEW IF HAVE NOT READ T-D)*

*(IF HAVE READ SUNDAY TIMES-DISPATCH):*

7. How many issues of the Sunday *Times-Dispatch* would you say you read during the past four weeks?

   18-1( ) One issue
     2( ) Two issues
     3( ) Three issues
     4( ) Four issues

There are four different types of news: local, state, national, and international. I'm going to read these types two at a time. As I read each pair, please tell me which type of news you read more of in the newspaper. *(READ AND ROTATE)*

8. 19-1( ) International news vs. Local news .....2( )
9. 20-1( ) Local news .... vs. State news ......2( )
10. 21-1( ) State news ..... vs. National news ...2( )
11. 22-1( ) National news .. vs. International news 2( )
12. 23-1( ) Local news .... vs. National news ...2( )
13. 24-1( ) International news vs. State news ......2( )

14. Do you ever read international news stories about poorer, economically underdeveloped countries such as Bangladesh, Thailand, Nigeria, and Peru?

   25-1( ) Yes
     2( ) No  *(SKIP TO QUESTION 18)*

15. When you read about these Third World countries, how much of the text do you generally read: *(READ AND ROTATE)*

    26-3( ) All or almost all of the text
    2( ) Half or more than half but not all
    1( ) Less than half of the text

16. When you read stories concerning economic development in poorer countries, do you generally read: *(READ AND ROTATE)*

    27-3( ) All or almost all of the text
    2( ) Half or more than half but not all
    1( ) Less than half of the text

17. What about stories on political events in poorer countries? Do you generally read: *(READ AND ROTATE)*

    28-3( ) All or almost all of the text
    2( ) Half or more than half but not all
    1( ) Less than half of the text

18. Do you agree or disagree that economic growth and progress in these poorer countries affect economics in Virginia?

    29-3( ) Agree
    1( ) Disagree

*(INTERVIEWER CHECK BELOW IF APPROPRIATE, BUT DO NOT ASK)*

    2( ) Neither agree nor disagree/No opinion

19. Do you agree or disagree that political and social upheavals in these poorer countries affect Virginians?

    30-3( ) Agree
    1( ) Disagree

*(INTERVIEWER CHECK BELOW IF APPROPRIATE, BUT DO NOT ASK)*

    2( ) Neither agree nor disagree/No opinion

20. Recently, there has been a great deal of talk about the interdependence of countries and that what happens in one country influences other countries. Do you agree or disagree that what happens in one country influences another country?

    31-3( ) Agree
    1( ) Disagree

*(INTERVIEWER CHECK BELOW IF APPROPRIATE, BUT DO NOT ASK)*

    2( ) Neither agree nor disagree/No opinion

21. Do you think it is important or not important to understand what is going on in poorer countries?

    32-3(    ) Important
    1(    ) Not important

*(INTERVIEWER CHECK BELOW IF APPROPRIATE, BUT DO NOT ASK)*

    2(    ) Neither important nor unimportant/No opinion

22. Do you think it is important or not important that newspapers provide more news about what is going on in poorer countries?

    33-3(    ) Important
    1(    ) Not important

*(INTERVIEWER CHECK BELOW IF APPROPRIATE, BUT DO NOT ASK)*

    2(    ) Neither important nor unimportant/No opinion

Now just a few simple questions to help make this survey more meaningful.

23a. How about where you live? Do you live in the city of Richmond, or in Chesterfield, Hanover, or Henrico County?

    34-1(    ) City of Richmond    4(    ) Henrico County
    2(    ) Chesterfield County    5(    ) Other  _____
    3(    ) Hanover County    9(    ) DK/NA

b. If you are currently employed, what kind of work do you do?

35-36 _____

*(IF RESPONDENT IS NOT EMPLOYED OR DOES NOT WORK,*
*DETERMINE STATUS)*

*PLEASE CHECK:*
    13(    ) Housewife
    14(    ) Student
    15(    ) Retired
    16(    ) Unemployed, looking for a job
    17(    ) Other _____    99(    ) DK/NA

c. What was the last grade of school you completed?

    37-1(    ) Part high school or less
    2(    ) High school graduate
    3(    ) Technical, vocational training/Part college
    4(    ) College graduate or more    9(    ) NA

d. In order to include all races in our survey, please tell me whether you are black, white, or a member of some other racial group?

38-1( ) Black
2( ) White
3( ) Other 9( ) NA

e. What is your marital status?

39-1( ) Now married
2( ) Widowed
3( ) Divorced or separated
4( ) Single (never married) 9( ) NA

f. In total, how many persons now live in your household, including children?

40-41( ) _____ Number

g. Would you consider yourself more (ROTATE) liberal or more conservative politically?

42-1( ) Liberal 3( ) Neither
2( ) Conservative 9( ) DK/NA

h. What is your religious preference? Is it (ROTATE) Protestant, Catholic, Jewish, some other faith, or do you have no preference?

43-1( ) Protestant
2( ) Catholic
3( ) Jewish
4( ) Some other faith
5( ) Have no preference 9( ) NA

i. Just approximately into which of these groups does the combined annual income for all members of your household fall?

44-1( ) Less than $20,000
2( ) $20,000 - $34,999
3( ) $35,000 - $49,999
4( ) $50,000 or more 9( ) NA

j. This is the last question. Some people use their given first names. Some use nicknames. What name do you go by at home?

_____

Thank you. You have been very helpful.

*INTERVIEWER, PLEASE CHECK:* 45-1( ) Male 2( ) Female

1-2 Card #

3-6 Case #

Telephone #

Respondent's
First Name
(if known)

Telephone Questionnaire

ANALYSIS OF NEWSPAPER REPORTING
ON DEVELOPING COUNTRIES

(Posttest)

Hello. This is _____ of _____.
May I please speak with _____?

*(IF SAME PERSON, CONTINUE INTERVIEW. IF PERSON NAMED IS
UNAVAILABLE, ASK WHAT WOULD BE A GOOD TIME TO CALL BACK:
_____. IF PERSON NAMED IS CALLED TO PHONE,
READ ABOVE INTRODUCTION AND CONTINUE INTERVIEW.)*

We talked with you recently and asked you some questions about newspaper
stories. At that time you said that you are a reader of the Sunday *Times-
Dispatch.* Is that correct? *(PAUSE)* We're asking the people who participated
in our survey to answer just a *few* follow-up questions, and would appreciate
a little more of your time.

For these first questions, please think specifically about poorer, economically
underdeveloped countries such as Bangladesh, Taiwan, Chad, and Brazil.

*(IF AT ANY POINT RESPONDENT ASKS WHETHER THESE ARE THE SAME
QUESTIONS HE/SHE HAS ALREADY ANSWERED, RESPOND:* "Yes, some
of the questions are the same. We want to see if your attitudes and opinions
have changed over time.")

    1. Do you agree or disagree that economic growth and progress in these
poorer countries affect economics in Virginia?

        9-3(    ) Agree
        1(    ) Disagree

*(INTERVIEWER CHECK BELOW IF APPROPRIATE, BUT DO NOT ASK)*

        2(    ) Neither agree nor disagree/No opinion

    2. Do you agree or disagree that political and social upheavals in these
poorer countries affect Virginians?

        10-3(    ) Agree
        1(    ) Disagree

*(INTERVIEWER CHECK BELOW IF APPROPRIATE, BUT DO NOT ASK)*

 2( ) Neither agree nor disagree/No opinion

3. Recently, there has been a great deal of talk about the interdependence of countries and that what happens in one country influences other countries. Do you agree or disagree that what happens in one country influences another country?

 11-3( ) Agree
 1( ) Disagree

*(INTERVIEWER CHECK BELOW IF APPROPRIATE, BUT DO NOT ASK)*

 2( ) Neither agree nor disagree/No opinion

4. Do you think it is important or not important to understand what is going on in poorer countries?

 12-3( ) Important
 1( ) Not important

*(INTERVIEWER CHECK BELOW IF APPROPRIATE, BUT DO NOT ASK)*

 2( ) Neither important nor unimportant/No opinion

5. Do you think it is important or not important that newspapers provide more news about what is going on in poorer countries?

 13-3( ) Important
 1( ) Not important

*(INTERVIEWER CHECK BELOW IF APPROPRIATE, BUT DO NOT ASK)*

 2( ) Neither important nor unimportant/No opinion

6. Did you happen to read the Sunday *Times-Dispatch* this past Sunday, or not?

 14-1( ) Yes
 2( ) No *(END INTERVIEW HERE)*

Thank you. You have been very helpful.

*(IF DID READ, CONTINUE INTERVIEW)*

*(READ SLOWLY)*

Today (this past Sunday), the *Times-Dispatch* ran a feature called "The Third World Comes Home...Real Measure of Trade Wars is in Powerful Effect on Lives," in which there were two stories: "Leaf-related firms' choice: export or die" and "Blackstone pays price as Brazil wins." Some people don't notice stories of this kind at all, some notice them but don't read them, and some read them.

178

7a. Did you happen to notice the story headlined ''Leaf-related firms' choice: export or die'' about the export of Virginia-made machinery used in the tobacco industry to Third World countries, and how this market affects jobs for Virginians?

15-1( ) Yes
2( ) No *(SKIP TO QUESTION 8a)*

*(IF ''YES'' ABOVE)*

b. How much, if any, of the text did you read? Did you read:

16-3( ) All or almost all of the text
2( ) Half or more than half but not all
1( ) Less than half of the text
9( ) None of the text

8a. What about the story headlined ''Blackstone pays price as Brazil wins'' on Virginia's declining shoe industry, due largely to the import of shoes from Third World countries such as Brazil? Did you happen to notice this story?

17-1( ) Yes
2( ) *(SKIP TO QUESTION 9)*

*(IF ''YES'' ABOVE)*

b. How much, if any, of the text did you read? Did you read:

18-3( ) All or almost all of the text
2( ) Half or more than half but not all
1( ) Less than half of the text
9( ) None of the text

*(IF READ EITHER OR BOTH STORIES, ASK QUESTION 9.*
*IF RESPONDENT READ NEITHER STORY, END INTERVIEW HERE)*

9. This is the last question. Now that you've read this type story, would you like to see more stories of this kind in the newspaper in the future, or not?

19-1( ) Yes
2( ) No
9( ) DK/NA

Thank you. You have been very helpful.

# Appendix 3

# Bringing the Third World To the College Classroom

### By Edward P. Bassett
Dean, Medill School of Journalism
Northwestern University

If *Main Street America and the Third World* does nothing more than encourage journalism instructors to convince aspiring journalists of the importance of foreign events, it will have been a success. But this book can do more: It can teach students how to report about developing nations in their first jobs, typically in small media markets. Moreover, this volume is an ideal resource for classes in other disciplines—in international relations and economics, for example—where American connections to the rest of the world should also be studied.

I know this from personal experience. As an experiment at the Medill School of Journalism, Assistant Professor Patricia Thompson and I used our sections of Advanced Reporting to introduce the concepts in this volume. This appendix relates that experience and the lessons learned.

The Advanced Reporting course, restricted to upperclassmen and generally peopled by seniors, seeks to develop students' reporting skills to a higher degree. It aims beyond routine event reporting and focuses on depth, research, polling, investigation, and specialized reporting. There are a number of assigned writing projects in the course. Some of the lectures and conferences prepare students for those projects. Other lectures examine issues and problems faced by today's reporters and readers. The course involves a number of readings to help the student develop a greater awareness of the journalism profession.

The course syllabus includes refreshers in interviewing techniques; the use of libraries and the state's Open Records Act; the development of sources; the use of polling data; and basic tax, budget, business, and finance issues.

Projects in the Advanced Reporting class are

—an assigned story that requires quick research in readily available news sources;

—a profile of the student's home community based on census data and written as a feature story for readers not familiar with the town;

—a class telephone survey and a publishable story written from the collected data;

—an in-depth story on a topic assigned by the instructor in the style of a *Chicago Tribune* TEMPO story, a *Washington Post* Style story, or the kind of piece found on the front page of *The Wall Street Journal*;

—a story on a local city government meeting;

—an editing assignment; and

—a final project that can be handled one of two ways: as an in-depth reporting project with a local publication or as an independent project approved by the instructor. Each approved project should be in one of the areas discussed during the quarter— for example, housing or transportation.

The *Main Street America and the Third World* approach can fit into several categories. Census data, for instance, provide statistics on foreign-born residents. Some students used this assignment to introduce "other world" angles to their stories. We encouraged students, however, to do Third World stories in their final projects. It was satisfying to see substantial numbers of students gravitate toward these themes.

Journalism instructors at several other universities have made tentative efforts to experiment with local Third World reporting based on the techniques in this book. Dr. John Fett, professor of agriculture journalism at the University of Wisconsin, for example, asked students to look for such stories; Dr. Dennis R. Jones and Dr. Arthur J. Kaul, at the School of Communication, the University of Southern Mississippi, had students write stories parallel to those prepared by the *Hattiesburg American*. Those initial steps revealed that the success of such assignments depends on adequately preparing students for a topic about which many are woefully unprepared.

To overcome this, we decided that students needed an overview outlining why Third World events are important to Americans and assuring them that they could report on those events locally. Our initial strategy was to bring in Jack Hamilton to meet with the class each quarter. During his presentation, an integral part of the syllabus, he explained the project and outlined various approaches. His general method was to get the students to draw on their own experience and inquisitiveness to start thinking of stories that might work in the community.

With the publication of this book, Hamilton's visits are no longer necessary. Students can read the introduction and selected stories ahead of time. The instructor can lead a discussion. Instructors may also wish to show "Connections: The Third World," the series put together by WSAZ-TV in Huntington, W. Va. Those tapes are available through the Society of Professional Journalists. Another way to enhance thinking about U.S.-Third World interdependence is to bring in a local figure who has business ties to the Third World. This may be best done in a second session on Third World topics, so that the students are prepared to ask good questions.

Our experience makes clear that students can ask the right questions and produce interesting stories, many of which introduce students to areas in the community that are otherwise ignored. The students were able, in fact, to go beyond merely copying the stories that Hamilton outlined or that appear in this book. One student prepared a story on the university's investments in Third World countries.

A second wrote a piece on tourist travel to Egypt. Although she had visited the country herself, she relied on local sources— for instance, a travel bureau and university scholars. Most important, she took the story into other issues besides travel, showing how important American tourism is to the troubled Egyptian economy and how Egypt's economic troubles make it less able to play a stabilizing role in the Middle East peace process. Certainly, those Americans who read such a story would better understand conditions in developing countries.

Instructors should not allow students to take on stories that are too general in nature. They should recognize that the subject matter is almost always new. It helps to build longer lead times into the assignments and to suggest sources that a student can contact.

As easy as we've found it to work within the Advanced Reporting class setting, there are a number of other ways in which journalism instructors can use these Third World reporting techniques.

Our school operates the Medill News Service in Washington, D.C. During their quarter in Washington, graduate students in print and broadcast sequences actually produce material for newspapers and television stations, which pay a monthly fee to the school for the service. The central idea is to shape national stories for hometown readers.

Charles Alexander, who directs the service, introduced a Main Street International beat for print students in 1986 with good results. The student assigned to the beat is expected to look at issues related to any country, not just those in the developing world. But Third World angles have proved fruitful and, in any case, the same techniques apply.

Stories have ranged from one on increased textile imports as a result of the Caribbean Basin Initiative (for the *Anderson Independent-Mail* in South Carolina) to another on Wisconsin investments in Ecuador—a piece tied to a Washington visit by Ecuador's president. (The Medill News Service has three client newspapers in Wisconsin.)

Several graduate students working for Hamilton as research assistants used information they found for stories of their own. Among the most interesting was one on the increase in patents registered in the United States by people from developing countries, a story that went to all Medill News Service newspapers.

The possibilities for using the techniques in this book in other courses are wide. Having students make a survey of their own connections or using the material to prepare research papers analyzing local issues can provide a world view that is too often missed in education. We think that world view is so important we have made the Third World reporting approach a regular part of our Advanced Reporting class syllabus.

## About the Author

*John Maxwell Hamilton*, who began his journalism career on *The Milwaukee Journal*, has reported from Washington, D.C., Latin America, the Middle East, and Africa, contributing to a variety of newspapers and magazines as well as ABC Radio. He has served with the U.S. Agency for International Development, specializing on Asian development issues; the House Foreign Affairs Committee, specializing on nuclear non-proliferation; and the World Bank. He has a Ph.D. in American Civilization from George Washington University and is a visiting professor in the Medill School of Journalism, Northwestern University.